# Healthy Lifestyle **Cookbook**

## A delicious guide to vegetarian cooking

by

*Paul Dallaghan and Jessica Blanchard*

ISBN: 978-616-90418-0-1

Third edition 2012
Second edition 2009
First edition 2008

Printed and bound in Thailand by Samui Aksorn Printing

**Samahita Retreat**
55/23 Moo 4 Namuang
Koh Samui
Surat Thani 84140
Thailand

**www.yoga-thailand.com**
**www.wellness-thailand.com**

# CONTENTS

**Acknowledgements and Gratitude** ..... i
**Foreword by Sri O. P. Tiwari** ..... ii

**Introduction** ..... 1
Yoga Thailand and Samahita Wellness ..... 3
Yoga, Health and Your Diet… ..... 4
A Personal Approach to Food and Yoga ..... 5
Guide to Optimal Diet, Digestion and Elimination ..... 5
The Core Ingredients ..... 14
**Essentials from India** ..... 15
Ghee ..... 15
Chapatis ..... 16
Caffeine-Free Chai ..... 17
Milk Rice ..... 18
**How to Make a Vegetarian Thai Curry Paste?** ..... 19
Green Curry Paste ..... 20
Massman Curry Paste ..... 21
Yellow Curry Paste ..... 22
**Thai Curries** ..... 23
Green Curry ..... 24
Penang Coconut Curry ..... 25
Massaman Curry ..... 26
"Kanom Jeen" Thai Yellow Curry with Rice Noodles ..... 27
"Gaeng Tay Pho" Thai Tamarind Curry with Morning Glory ..... 28
**Tofu Dishes** ..... 29
"Haw Mok" Steamed Tofu in Banana Leaves ..... 30
"Laab" Tofu ..... 31
Coconut Curry Tofu ..... 32
Ginger Malay Tofu ..... 33
Spicy Curry Tofu ..... 34
Sweet and Sour Tofu ..... 35
Tofu Burger ..... 36
**Soups** ..... 37
"Tom Kha" Coconut Lemongrass Soup ..... 38
Minestrone Soup ..... 39
Winter Melon Vegetable Soup ..... 40
"Tom Yum" Vegetable Soup ..... 41
Pumpkin Soup ..... 42
"Rassam" Indian Tomato Soup ..... 43
Indian Mixed Vegetable Soup ..... 44
**Bean & Lentil Recipes** ..... 45
Sprouted Mung Falafel with Yoghurt Sauce ..... 46
Kitcheri ..... 47
Sprouted Mung Beans ..... 48
South-Indian Mung Beans ..... 49
Yellow Mung Dahl Soup ..... 50
Vegetarian Chili ..... 51

Indian Red Bean Soup ........ 52
Brazilian Black Bean Soup ........ 53
**Noodles** ........ 55
Glass Noodle Stir Fry ........ 56
Pad Thai ........ 57
Pad See Eiw ........ 58
Mee Gorang Noodles ........ 59
Sattvic Pesto Pasta ........ 60
**Rice** ........ 61
Vegetarian Sushi ........ 62
Veggie Stir Fried Rice ........ 63
Orange & Veggie Couscous ........ 64
Indian Lemon Rice ........ 65
Indian Tomato Rice ........ 66
**Vegetables** ........ 67
Mixed Vegetable with Ginger Stir Fry ........ 68
Kale Stir fry ........ 69
Oven-Roasted Vegetables ........ 70
Pumpkin Stir Fry ........ 71
Steamed Vegetables ........ 72
Indian Vegetable Subji ........ 73
Chickpea & Cauliflower Subji ........ 74
Indian-Style Potatoes with Tomatoes ........ 75
Potato & Green Bean Subji ........ 76
**Salad and Dressings** ........ 77
Vietnamese Summer Rolls ........ 78
Sweet Potato Salad ........ 79
"Som Tom" Thai Papaya Salad ........ 80
"Yam Yai" Thai Green & Veggie Salad ........ 81
Cucumber, Coconut & Mung Salad ........ 82
Carrot, Coconut & Sprout Salad ........ 83
Vinaigrette Salad Dressing ........ 84
Black Sesame Dressing ........ 84
Simple Olive Oil Dressing ........ 85
Tahini Lime Dressing ........ 85
**Desserts** ........ 87
Mango Sticky Rice ........ 88
Energy Balls ........ 89
Swedish Choco-Oat Balls ........ 90
Cashew Nut Cup ........ 91
Guilt-Free Chocolate Balls ........ 92
Blueberry Crumble ........ 93
Choc-Oat Chip Cookies ........ 94
Whole Wheat Shortbread Cookies ........ 95
Vegan Cookies ........ 96
"The Best Ever Carrot Cake" ........ 97
"All Equal Cake" ........ 98
Yoghurt Cake ........ 99
Vegan Chocolate Cake ........ 100

# Acknowledgements and Gratitude

We would both like to thank our parents who brought us up on good, wholesome, home cooked food. Without such an influence it would be hard to offer it here. Additional recipes were offered by Jutima's mother, an experienced chef living in Atlanta. Paul's mother and sister also offered some of their recipes that we grew up with.

We would also like to thank all of the chef's that we have worked closely with over the years, especially Chef Su and her key assistant Khun Rung. The whole effort is a team approach from the juice bar to the kitchen with Yao, Nee, Bon, Pick, Gop, Bhu, Ohm, Goi and Mam.

We must also thank Sandya, our Indian mama, who was part of Samahita Retreat in the first few years and brought her great recipes and cooking skills to us. She is still the most popular cook for yoga students in Mysore, India today.

Also many thanks to Jessica Blanchard for getting this process started by compiling the recipes and making this cookbook a physical reality.

Pictures say a thousand words. The food photos are courtesy of Lynn Mutchler and Cortnee Brown, who worked tirelessly turning these pictures into art. Other photo credits go to some of our friends who are also talented photographers; Mikko Seppinen, Sandra D Bianco and Vilhelm Sjostrom.

There have also been a number of helpful, skilled and innovative students over the years who have shared their treats and subsequently became part of the Samahita Retreat food offering. Thank you all.

This cookbook has grown out of repeated requests for the recipes of what we cook and serve at Samahita Retreat. After many earlier versions we are delighted to bring out this latest edition to hopefully serve as a resource for all those interested.

We are fully aware of and grateful to the support of the Divine Energy in making it all happen.

**Enjoy!**
**Paul & Jutima Dallaghan, Founders Samahita Retreat**
**Yoga Thailand - Centered Yoga - Wellness Thailand**

*Paul and Jutima live in Koh Samui, Thailand with their two sons, Sean and Dylan.*

# **Foreword** *by Sri O. P. Tiwari*

This new book on cooking is special in the sense it tries to cover whatever defines healthy food from a vegetarian-cum-yogic point of view. You will notice that all the recipes are for vegetarian cooking. The reason for this is very well said by Colin Campbell in his book The China Study:

> *"Slowly truth is emerging that diet is decisive to health out of a fog of deliberate confusion and fierce resistance put up by the food and pharmaceutical industries and their allies in government, academia and big medicine. The idea is winning support in the public mind and a new picture is emerging and it is becoming clear. The picture is that the diet centered on animal products, meat, dairy and eggs is actually toxic and promotes all the main chronic diseases; cardiovascular, cancer, diabetes, obesity and auto-immune that cause death in U.S. and other industrialized countries."*

In the field of yoga we do not emphasize the content of the food; instead we look at how it affects our mind and body. As is said in the Shrimad Bhagavad Gita, food is of three types. Rajasic, which makes one hyper-active or sensitive, gives rise to anger, greed, fear and creates ambivalence. Second type of food is Tamasic; that which makes you lethargic, non-active, dull and lazy. It creates a sluggish liver and spleen, brings down the blood pressure and disturbs the thyroid function. Third type of food is energetic, called Sattvic, light to digest, creates balance in the doshas and develops emotional stability.

This book is written from the point of view of how to create a Sattvic balance in your Doshas.

It may not consider caloric value but it certainly takes good care of ingredients to be used with particular preparation of food. In the Hatha Pradipika (chapter 1, verse 63), one of the foremost works on hatha yoga, it is said:

> *pushtam samadhuram snigdham gavyam dhatu praposanam /*
> *manobhilashitam yogyam yogi bhojanamacharet //*
>
> *The yogi should eat nourishing food, combined with ghee, it should be nutritious but also tasty*
> *So it is liked and can be fully digested promoting growth in practices and yoga.*

Typically we prefer to eat what was fed to us during childhood. Some likes and dislikes exist based on our samskaras, our previous patterns. We can recondition but should never be caught by a rigid attitude. The quest must be to search for what suits us and what does not. If this is the attitude then we can find the basic foods we need most to enable our growth.

I am confident this cookbook from Samahita Retreat will serve the above purpose, give insight to the users and benefit them physically and psychologically. Yet more, a foundation will be laid down for spiritual growth.

My blessings to Jutima and Paul, who make a wonderful and devoted couple, which comes through in the care taken in both this book and their center, Samahita Retreat.

> *Sri Om Prakash Tiwari is a master yogi, a disciple of Swami Kuvalyananda, a pioneer in yoga and science over the past century. Tiwairiji directs the Kaivalyadham Institute, Lonavla, India. He carries both the traditional, classical yogic training plus the modern, scientific outlook with him. He is one of the few remaining masters who thoroughly understands the nature and practice of pranayama through direct personal experience and the passing on of the tradition through the lineage of his teacher and that before him. Paul is one of the senior students of Tiwariji trained in this path with a major emphasis on pranayama. The nature of food and its effect on us is crucial to yoga and so this emphasis continues through these teachings, this book and the center.*

**Sri Om Prakash Tiwari,** *Kaivalyadham, Lonavla, India, June 2009*

# Introduction

Tiwariji and Paul, morning fire ceremony at Samahita Retreat

# Introduction

The importance of food in relation to yoga and its practices cannot be overstated. A very clear description given of yoga is "the science of experience and the art of living". We start to see that yoga is more than just the physical postures done on a yoga mat and more about our behavior and how we treat others and ourselves. The body affects the mind and vice versa. Whatever we put in our system affects the functioning of our consciousness.

We learn from the ancient teachings and wisdom of genuine yogis what is good for our systems in the practice of yoga and what will hinder that growth. Food is emphasized as one of the most important factors. Since the beginning of Samahita Retreat we have placed key attention on the preparation, quality and taste of the food served.

Yoga traditionally recommends food that is 'sattvic', which basically means pure, fresh, easy to digest and leaves you feeling clear and light. This should be the result of eating, not feeling heavy, dull or agitated. For food to be properly digested and benefit us the psychological aspect plays a large role. Taste is the primary aspect to affect your like or dislike of it. If the food is not tasty then it's not sattvic.

As we become more aware of our thoughts, feelings and actions, aided through continued yoga practice, we see more and more the effect of food on our mind and body. The food we take will either aid or hinder our growth. Quite literally our choice of food can make or break our practice of yoga.

Taking all this to heart, the benefit and enjoyment of food is an integral part of Samahita Retreat. The food presented in this book is not only for a practitioner of yoga. It is healthy, clean and tasty and to the benefit of all regardless of background or lifestyle, for the yogi's diet is nourishing, light and tasty, a key to good health through food no matter who you are.

This compilation is a collection of recipes served at Samahita Retreat over the years. Our food has always been home cooked with much care and joy. This is also a vital ingredient in any meal. It changes the energetic vibration and adds to the tasty and nourishing qualities of the food. Through this publication we hope you can experience the same in your own home.

The majority of our recipes are vegetarian and without garlic or onion but feel free to add these to your cooking if you wish. Eating like this over a long period of time, you start to notice the positive effects within. We wish the utmost health of mind and body for you.

## Dedicated Yoga and Wellness Center

Samahita Retreat was established with a specific purpose in mind – as a venue for practicing yoga and learning healthy and positive living habits. As such, it provides an ideal environment in which to learn, experience, and practice the lessons imparted in our courses. Few such places exist in the modern world.

At Samahita Retreat we cultivate a friendly, comfortable environment that allows guests to be social or private, according to their liking. With excellent facilities at their disposal, guests have the option of engaging in a variety of practices and treatments during their stay. We have made a special effort to maintain eco-friendly standards throughout the entire property.

Our Samahita Wellness Center offers a complete approach to well-being, one that takes into account physical, spiritual, emotional, and mental aspects of one's health. We believe all these factors contribute to wellness and thus take a holistic approach to living a healthy life.

Food has a tremendous effect on our body, mind, and consciousness, so this is one area we take care of immediately. We go to great lengths to serve carefully prepared meals that nourish inside and out, most of which are presented in this cookbook.

We also offer several cleansing programs, which can take your yoga practice a step further while transforming your body and mind. We are equipped to take you through a full detox program followed by guidance on how to continue living in a way that supports you, your body, and your mind. The aim is that you leave Samahita Retreat empowered, whether or not you are a practitioner of yoga. Our Healthy weight program has been designed to help your return your body to its natural weight and our De-stress Program allows you to mentally 'detox' from modern living and nature your body and mind through healthy eating, rejuvenating therapies and a relaxation in a healing enviroment.

Samahita Retreat lies on the south coast of Koh Samui, a tropical island in the Gulf of Thailand that has long stretches of pristine beaches and unspoiled land. Only about an hour away from Bangkok by air, an hour and a half from Singapore, and three hours from Hong Kong, Samui has the allure of a remote island paradise but with the accessibility of the region's most popular destinations.

# Yoga, Health and Your Diet

The intrinsic message of yoga is to remove "un-well". It is a completely holistic approach taking into account our physical, psychological, mental and spiritual state. In a sense, the achievement of yoga is perfect balance, all artificiality removed, our true nature shining forth, overall wellness predominating.

Yoga offers many tools and techniques of practice to achieve this balance, and wellbeing. It is impossible to separate the physical from the psychological as they are always interlinked. So an approach to taking care of the body is integrated with control and mastery of the mind and senses.

One of the key teachings in yoga is how to manage food with the key advice being "eat in moderation", never over eat nor starve yourself unnecessarily. Additionally, food has a tremendous emotional impact. Modern nutrition is also very strongly focused on food for health. Both systems of yoga and modern nutrition apply techniques to maintain strength and vigor of body along with a positive mental state.

In order to move further in the field of inner growth and peace of mind, the state of the body and subsequently its diet must be looked at. In a modern world we come across so much abuse of food on a personal and global level. Much food is wasted in one area while others go hungry elsewhere. Even in the land of the plenty the modern state of food has led to a form of under-nourishment as the quality and composition of food has vastly deteriorated and moved away from its natural state. So today we have to navigate a mix of processed and refined foods along with chemically structured and polluted foods. With modern lifestyle being so pressured and stressed we will typically take the simplest solution available.

As a result we find our level of "un-well" increased as we are stressed and improperly fed. This makes it difficult to progress internally and can leave us dissatisfied in day-to-day life. Our observation over years of teaching yoga is that people's digestion and elimination is out of balance, their intake is over active (meaning their consumption of food and other items) with much of it based on habits and cravings and a lack of discipline. In the language of yoga, both "prana" and "apana" malfunction, keeping one away from the "yoga". But that is how it works today. We are not educated on how to breathe correctly and which foods can benefit us most, or the quality of the water we should be drinking. So it is the responsibility of the field of yoga and wellness to inform, educate and empower. We consider it our direct duty to offer this.

An initial step in yoga is cleaning out in order to build up our system, at first physically but ultimately mentally. Based on our diet and lifestyle we might need much more than just a few asana practices a week. In fact, one can feel blocked and unable to make progress while doing the asanas as the bodily system is having a hard time detoxifying. The combination of modern food types leaves a residue of undigested matter, "ama" as it is termed in ayurveda, in our system. We feel heavy, stiff, lethargic and experience poor concentration and dissatisfaction with life. To regularly do a yoga practice is important but help from a focused detox program is a needed boost, almost a required step. It should be supplemented with education on how to take care of yourself through diet, physical practices and keeping up a mental well-being.

> *"He who takes medicine and neglects to diet wastes the skill of his doctors."*
> ***- Chinese Proverb***

This leaves yoga and wellness inevitably interlinked. The body is nature's greatest gift. May we take care of it. In so doing, there is a natural impact on our psychological state, our peace of mind. And the only way to achieve it is to work on ourselves.

# A Personal Approach to Food and Yoga

Food has a great effect on both your body and mind. It can make or break your inner development, the yoga process within you. So many blunders are committed in the realm of food. If you watch what goes in the mouth (i.e. eating) and what comes out of the mouth (i.e. talking) you have taken care of 80% of yogic practice and living. The Hatha (Yoga) Pradipika constantly emphasizes these two points to practitioners. So much of it comes down to your own will power, the control over the tongue.

> *"True happiness is impossible without true health and true health is impossible without rigid control of the palate. All the other senses will automatically come under our control when the palate has been brought under control. And he who has conquered his senses has really conquered the whole world."*
>
> ***- Gandhi***

The physical body is the combined effect of the food you eat and the interaction with the oxygen breathed in. There is truth in the statement "you are what you eat", at least as far as the physical body is concerned. Yet the yoga teachings reveal, and experience will show you, that food creates thought. So, some foods (sattvic) will either encourage a calm, clear state of mind while others can throw the system and mind into such an agitated (rajasic) or dull (tamasic) state, such as the effects from alcohol, strong stimulative foods, or heavy, stale and dull foods.

> *"Food makes thinking possible. Therefore the right food is of paramount importance. You must eat when you are in a cheerful mood. Do not overload the stomach. By the purity of food, follows the purification of the inner nature."*
>
> ***- Swami Sivananda***

Food is a source of habit and upbringing so you should not force a particular way of eating or certain food types on yourself. The real need is to find the right approach to eating. We have formed bad habits over the years that need addressing if health and mental wellbeing are to be prolonged and cultivated. You do not have to be a vegetarian to practice yoga though you might gradually move to that diet over time. The opening statement of the Yoga Sutras uses the word "anushaasanam". It implies that growth must arise within you, not forced upon you, though discipline is required. Yoga and meditative practices lead to a subtle development, an inner lightening, out of which may arise a desire for a cleaner, vegetarian diet. Yet eating a cleaner, balanced diet will also help one purify, strengthen and grow.

> *"Nothing will benefit human health and increase the chances for survival of life on Earth as much as the evolution to a vegetarian diet."*
>
> ***- Albert Einstein***

Food should support your personal practice and how you live. It should be enjoyable and tasty. **Hippocrates** uttered the now famous words *"Let thy food be thy medicine."* We take food not just as a preventative medicine to aid the physical body but as a tool in itself to aid in the growth of consciousness, healing in the process our "avidya", delusion and ignorance, the ill of "samsara", conditioned existence. Food is part of practice.

**We would like to offer a few underlying principles to aid your food decisions:**

***Natural, fresh and simple in a moderate quantity with full respect to your food***

## 1. Quality of Food should be Natural, Fresh and Simple – "Sattvic"

***Natural*** and organic (where possible these days) grown food, minimal to zero processing. This really means nothing from a can, plastic pack or frozen meals, but as close to its original whole nature as is possible. Get your food as ***fresh*** to harvest date as is good for that food, especially vegetables and fruits. It is also helpful if it is locally produced. Try not to keep reheating food for days; this destroys its nutritional value. The best is to cook it fresh and eat it there and then.

It should be ***simple*** to prepare, simple to cook and simple to digest. This is key as we know how much time is spent cooking and so much organic bodily energy is used in digestion. A few key ingredients properly combined can be thoroughly nutritious, completely tasty when the right spices are added, and very easy to digest.

**The diet that we eat has an effect on our consciousness through the gunas!** Yoga practitioners can learn to observe the effects of different foods on the mind, those that make us feel heavy and lethargic and those that make us feel light and energetic.

Examples of Foods and the Gunas:

- Sattvic foods: fruits, vegetables (less so than fruits, especially those that grow on the ground), milk (organic), ghee, whole grains, especially wheat and basmati rice, mung beans, nuts, especially almonds, honey, cardamom, coriander, fennel, ginger
- Rajasic foods: onions, garlic, chilies, cayenne, cabbage family (mildly), kidney, soy beans (except mung and tofu), chocolate (also tamasic), alcohol, coffee
- Tamasic foods: meat, fish, eggs, mushrooms, seaweed, old, spoiled, stale foods, heavy foods, over eating, canned foods

## 2. Quantity of Food, "Mitahara" – Moderate Eating

Overeating, even of the purest food, will undo the benefit on your system energetically. You can gauge a moderate amount based on the level of your current activity. This requires a self-observing mind to learn from experience in how you feel after eating different quantities of food under the different circumstances. Traditional advice given says 'keep one fourth of your stomach empty to allow the gases to move'. More advice offers stopping 3-4 spoonfuls before you would normally consider to be satiated, or eating no more than two fully cupped hands of food.

> *"The heart is great which shows moderation in the midst of prosperity."*
>
> ***- Lucius Annaeus Seneca***

It is possible to get used to one full serving on your typical sized plate or bowl. Or use small bowls and regulate the quantity whilst eating slowly. You will need to carefully observe how much you take and what size dish helps you manage it. Some only eat once a day with milk or juice morning and night. Others will eat something in the morning, a good lunch and nothing to minimal at night. Key is definitely light at night, long before bed. Let the body properly repair whilst you sleep and may you feel light and fresh upon rising in the morning. You will find it easy to adapt to such an approach once you get started.

### 3. Develop a Loving, Respectful Relationship to Food

In terms of yoga or inner development your relationship with food, how you connect with it, is most important. Mindful eating is key. Before you begin to eat, silently, consciously feel the connection with the food. You can create an energetic loop from the food on your plate to your belly area then up through the heart, out the crown of the head and back to your food. Feel its vibration. This food you are eating is an offering of prana to the spirit within; the inner pranic flow. It is a sacred act. Try to feel each mouthful of food, entering, chewing and swallowing. Feel it reach the stomach. Enjoy it. Be mindful. Eat consciously. Even if sitting with others still try to keep the connection and feel it.

> *"There is a sufficiency in the world for man's need but not for man's greed."*
> ***- Gandhi***

***Never waste food.*** Many others go hungry in the world. Eat conscientiously. In fact the biggest way we can help world hunger is to prepare just enough food for us to eat without ever wasting. Perhaps just enough extra as an offering or to an unintended guest. The modern world has such a high wastage of food it is a crime against all beings. Many individuals in today's society have issues with eating and a poor relationship to food. Learning how to respect food and never waste it can cure so many personal psychological and social ills. All it takes is for us to be mindful, conscientious and aware, with a feeling for our hungry brothers. Herein the growth of compassion is sown by our own direct selfless action.

**Remember, we eat to live, not live to eat.**

Sattva Dining at Samahita Retreat

# Guide to Optimal Diet, Digestion and Elimination

The key to long-term health is to find a way to remove the root cause of a toxic lifestyle and to incorporate detoxifying measures into your daily routine. The diet can either support good health or contribute to illness.

There are three major aspects that must be looked at

**A. Diet :** what goes in
**B. Digestion :** how it is broken down and assimilated
**C. Elimination :** what comes out

Finding a diet that encourages good digestion and assimilation of nutrients will facilitate the elimination of wastes and help to avoid constipation. By keeping our digestion working well, we build healthy tissues and avoid the production of toxins, that is, food that is absorbed into the system without being properly digested. The digestion is the process of transformation of food by the body into healthy tissues, with the elimination of waste produced in the process. Fire transforms materials, and we can think of our digestive power as a fire. The following tips will help to regulate digestion, and subsequently prevent the formation of disease while naturally purifying the body on a daily basis.

## A. Diet

***1. Favor foods in their whole form***
The less processing the better. A whole foods diet consisting of vegetables, fruits, whole grains, and legumes will keep your system healthy. Nature is very intelligent, and when we take the whole form of a food, it is naturally balanced to be used appropriately by our systems. For example, when you take the whole form of wheat it looks like a berry with a hard outer coating containing lots of fibre, with a starchier interior. When we take the whole berry, the fibre helps the starchier interior to be moved through our system. When wheat is refined we strip off the fibre and are left with pure starch, which sticks to the intestines like glue. The same applies to sugar: whole forms of sugar like brown sugar, maple syrup or molasses do not have the same detrimental effects on the system as white sugar. It disrupts the blood sugar, endocrine system and will increase fatigue and anxiety. It also ferments in the GI tract, causing acidity, and inflammatory symptoms, similar to alcohol. When foods are refined, they are stripped of nature's intelligence.

***2. Eliminate white sugar and white flour.***
You will feel much better as a result! As mentioned above, refined products disrupt the body's natural intelligence, and they offer little to no nutritional value. Always choose unrefined sugar and flour. When baking, you can substitute whole wheat, rye, spelt, or brown rice flour for white flour. You can substitute maple syrup, brown rice syrup, succonat, turbinado or raw sugar for white sugar. You can also use dried dates soaked in water as a sweetener in shakes or smoothies.

***3. Substitute animal protein (meat, eggs, chicken, fish, seafood) with plant sources of protein (legumes, beans, nuts, seeds).***
Animal proteins are heavy to digest, and accumulate more environmental toxins, which are stored in the fat of the animal. Plant sources of protein tend to be less polluted and cleaner burning fuels for the body. There is much controversy about the amount of protein needed in the diet. Whole grains and vegetables contain protein, although not as concentrated amounts as that found in animal products. We do not need to consume highly concentrated sources of protein, because eating a varied diet of whole grains, vegetables, nuts, seeds and beans will give us adequate protein. In fact, it is almost impossible NOT to get enough protein if you are following a diet of whole foods. The human body only needs about 2.5% of calories from protein, according to the American Journal of Clinical Nutrition. The World Health Organization sets the adult requirement at about 4.5 percent.

Protein from vegetable sources is a cleaner source of protein. When the body digests animal protein it produces uric acid, which can accumulate in the body, especially in weakened areas, such as the joints. Once the body is saturated with uric acid, it starts to migrate throughout the body, especially to the weaker areas, like the joints, causing pain and blockages (symptoms you may notice in your yoga practice). Over time it can cause arthritis, gout and other autoimmune disorders*. Uric acid also has a very negative effect on the pH of the body and the kidneys. All animal flesh is also very heavy for the body to digest, taking 48 to 72 hours to be processed, tending to sit in the intestines and cause toxic bacteria*.

* *Source: Perfect Balance: Ayurvedic Nutrition for your Mind, Body, and Soul, by Atreya Smith*

**4. *Watch coffee consumption (the less the better).***
Coffee is extremely acidic and taxing to the nervous system. It has been seen to make PMS (pre/menopausal symptoms) worse. Caffeine is probably the most widely used stimulant in the world. Many people are complete caffeine addicts. Coffee and tea both contain caffeine, however coffee comes from a bean, and tea from the tea plant. Their properties and chemical structures are completely different, so will be the effects on the body. Excessive caffeine consumption has similar effects – anxiety, nervousness, insomnia or disrupted sleep, stomach and intestinal maladies, and moodiness.

Harmful chemicals are used in the production of coffee, poisonous herbicide and pesticide sprays in its cultivation, petroleum-based solvents in the decaffeination (this is why it is very important to use steam-processed decaffeinated coffee). Coffee is acidic, and the acid in coffee over time can eat away at the villi of the small intestine, reducing its ability to absorb and assimilate the nutrients from food. Drinking two cups of nettle leaf tea per day for six weeks can repair coffee-damaged small intestines.

**5. *Limit alcohol.***
Alcohol is acidic, and therefore will simulate digestion in those with slow or sluggish digestion. Conversely, alcohol has a strong dulling effect on the mind, and will make it harder to make healthy dietary choices. Regular consumption of alcohol leads to the desire for other strong tastes in the diet like salt, meats, fats and refined sugar. It is fermented, and has a strong heating effect on the body. It will make the blood acidic and toxic.

**6. *Drink ginger tea.***
Ginger encourages digestion, intestinal motility, and draws toxins from the body. Although the taste of ginger is initially spicy, it has a sweet post-digestive effect on the body, making it rejuvenating and good for all constitutions. It is one of the best digestive stimulants, and it helps to move accumulations from the body. For this reason it is used as an anti-inflammatory agent in the treatment of rheumatoid arthritis. Drinking ginger tea on a daily basis will help you to maintain a balanced metabolism.

**7. *Eat full meals and limit snacking (only if actually hungry, not bored!)***
The body needs time to process each meal, and the digestive system needs a rest in between meals. If you are constantly snacking, your system does not have time to fully process one meal before it must work on the next. Constantly grazing will cause the accumulation of ama (toxins) in the system.

**8. *Drink warm/room temperature water with meals rather than iced drinks.***
Cold drinks put out the digestive fire, and encourage slow, sluggish digestion. When making smoothies or shakes, avoid adding ice; this makes them much harder to digest.

**9. *Weekly one day cleanse.***
One day per week eating a very light diet or having only juices will give your digestion a rest, and allow the body to de-toxify itself. It will also build up your digestive fire, and promote the elimination undigested food and toxins.

As a guide we recommend one day in week (or two weeks) take only:

- Fresh cooked vegetables
- Vegetable broth
- Vegetable soup
- Fruit
- No coffee, black tea, or alcohol
- Drink ginger tea, green tea or other herbal teas

You will feel lighter and brighter the next day. Doing this on a weekly basis, you will notice that your weight will naturally come to its correct place.

### 10. Include living foods in your diet.

Living foods, like sprouts and fresh vegetables, are still alive. They contain chlorophyll, antioxidants, and high levels of " prana" or life force. Sprouts are especially important, because they represent the stage of the seed when it has germinated and has the most life potential. During sprouting, vitamin and enzyme content increases dramatically. The sprouting process predigests the nutrients of the seed, making it easier to assimilate and metabolize, but also increases the cooling properties of the seed, which can be overly cool for someone with very low digestive fire. In winter the cooling properties of sprouts can be balanced by cooking them. Lightly steaming sprouts from larger grains like adzuki, lentil, soy and wheat make them easier to digest while still being energizing.

### 11. Wheatgrass as a supplement.

Wheatgrass contains very high levels of chlorophyll; higher levels than available in most other foods. It is cooling, and especially beneficial to those with inflammation or overly acidic states. Wheatgrass offers unique digestive enzymes not available in high concentration in other foods. The hundreds of enzymes they contain help resolve indigestible and toxic substances in food. They also contain high levels of antioxidants, which slow cellular deterioration and mutation and are useful in the treatment of degenerative disease and in the management of aging. It has also been used to improve and heal arthritis and inflammatory conditions. The carbohydrate structure of wheatgrass also has the ability to strengthen all body tissues, including the heart and arteries, lower blood fat and reduce inflammations. Fresh wheatgrass may not be available to you, however taking one teaspoon of freeze dried wheatgrass powder as a supplement can still give positive benefits.

### 12. Eliminate refined or hydrogenated oils and replace them with ghee, coconut oil, sesame oil, sun flower seed oil and olive oil.

Refined oils are the worst form of oil for the body, and release free radicals, which cause cellular damage and speed up the aging process. Use cold pressed, unrefined oils for cooking and salads. It is best not to heat poly or monounsaturated oils, because they also release an oxygen molecule when heated, which is a free radical. The best oils for cooking are sesame, coconut and ghee. These can be heated to high temperatures without oxidizing or becoming rancid. Olive oil, which is a very healthy fat, is better when taken raw. If you heat olive oil, it should not smoke and should be heated on low to medium.

According to Ayurveda, ghee enhances the essence that governs immunity, promotes resistance against disease, and the healing of injuries and gastro-intestinal inflammations such as ulcers and colitis. It also increases the digestive capacity and the body's ability to absorb nutrients from foods. Nutrition expert Rudolph Ballentine, M.D. (author of many books such as *Radical Healing, Transition to Vegetarianism*), found that clarified butter contains butyric acid, a fatty acid that has antiviral and anti-cancer properties, and which raises the level of the antiviral chemical, interferon, in the body. Butyric acid also has characteristics found to be helpful in the prevention and treatment of Alzheimer's disease. Interestingly, it is also a key anti-aging ingredient in many of the latest "all natural" beauty products.

## B. Digestion

The digestive process is of utmost importance to a person's health, because foods go directly to construct the tissues of the body. By keeping our digestion working well, we build healthy tissues and avoid the production of toxins (*ama*), food that is absorbed into the system without being properly digested. Partially digested material cannot be used by the system, and acts to clog it. *Ama* is generated by food that should go to form healthy tissue and instead becomes a substance that will nourish disease. Signs of ama in the body are a coated tongue, fatigue, especially after eating, bad breath, sticky or bad smelling stool, and stool which does not float.

If the digestion is working well, we will also be more likely to have regular eliminations, another key to health. The digestion is the process of transformation of food by the body into healthy tissues, with the elimination of waste produced in the process. Fire transforms materials, and we can think of our digestive power as a fire, called agni. By regulating the *agni*, we prevent the formation of disease, and naturally purify the body on a daily basis.

### Digestive Spices

The following spices will regulate the digestive fire by helping your body to produce the enzymes needed for digestion.

| Digestive spices for doshas | | |
|---|---|---|
| **Vata** | **Pitta** | **Kapha** |
| *Irregular digestion* | *Strong digestion* | *Slow digestion* |
| Cardamom | Cumin | Dry Ginger |
| Fennel | Fennel | Black Pepper |
| Cumin | Coriander | Cumin |
| | | Fenugreek |

Use the spices in a powdered form, mix the spices in equal quantity, take ½ teaspoon before meals. It is better to buy the seeds, then to use a coffee grinder to powder the spices. Powdered spices lose most of their medicinal properties after six months of grinding.

## C. Elimination

As the body digests and metabolizes, it produces wastes that are eliminated through the urinary tract, GI tract, and through the skin or sebaceous glands. The waste products of these channels are the urine, stool, and sweat. It is important that all three are working and eliminating on a daily basis.

If you are not passing stool on a daily basis, or the bowel movements are not complete, you can consider yourself constipated. This problem needs to be addressed, because when the stool stays in the system too long, toxins can be re-absorbed, and the waste products can ferment in the colon.

### Constipation Relief Tips

Often constipation is due to dryness in the colon, and/or a lack of peristaltic movement in the colon. In yogic terms, this is the movement of *apana vayu,* one of the five sub-classifications of vata dosha. Apana holds onto waste until the appropriate time, then eliminates it with a downward movement, like when passing stool, urinating, ejaculating, menstruating or giving birth. There are a number of reasons why Apana's movement can be disrupted, such as a change in schedule, travel, long term use of the birth control pill, or an excessively dry or vata aggravating diet. First, look at your diet, because digestion and elimination are interconnected. For elimination to work correctly, digestion must also be functioning well.

- **Simplify.** Encourage ease of digestion by keeping your food combinations simple. Avoid mixing more than 2-3 types of food. If you have muesli, have it with soy milk or warm milk, and do not add fruits. If you mix muesli with yoghurt, fruits, and nuts, you make your system work very hard at breakfast, when it is just getting started.
- **Eat fruits on their own,** then wait 20 minutes before consuming other foods.
- **Warm and wet.** Limit your consumption of raw foods, these are drying to the system. Cooking pre-digests foods for your system, consequently when you eat raw your system uses more of its own juices. Stick to salad greens with an oil dressing.
- **Unctuous.** Add more oils to your diet: ghee, olive oil, sesame oil, flax seed oil, and coconut oil are good sources. Coconut oil is a very good substitute for those who do not eat dairy. It has many good properties, including being anti-bacterial and anti-fungal. Nuts are also a good source of oil, however limit consumption to one handful at a time.
- **Fiber.** Ensure that you are getting enough whole grains, these give your intestines the bulk that they need to pass the food through the colon. Rice, wheat (especially without yeast, like chapattis), quinoa and oats are good. The dietary fiber in carbohydrates contains pre-biotics, the precursor to the production of pro-biotics, which are needed for your digestion.
- **Avoid dry foods** like crackers, popcorn, muesli. Soak dried fruits.
- **Simple.** Fresh vegetables are very good for health, however don't consume many different types of vegetables at one meal.
- **Soups, one-pot meals** are very good for encouraging lubrication and elimination.

As discussed above, the first step for encouraging good elimination is to look at the "digestive fire" or digestive process. If you are taking spices and have modified your diet and still experience constipation, there are a few remedies to consider.

**Triphala:** "Three fruits" – Triphala is a mix of Amla, Haritaki and Bibhitaki, three Indian fruits which all have medicinal properties, and become even more powerful when used together. Triphala is a rejuvenative to the colon, meaning that it helps to promote and correct its functioning. It is especially powerful when used to correct absorption problems. It can have a laxative effect, although it may not if you experience dryness in the colon. Take 1-2 teaspoons at night before bed.

**Castor Oil:** Castor oil is a gentle purgative, and is very good for its laxative effects, because it is heavy and oily; it doesn't imbalance the energetic movement of the body (Vata dosha). It has many medicinal uses, and is commonly used for treatment of arthritis in India. It removes ama (toxins) from the colon, and also removes excess doshas from the GI tract. As a laxative, the dose of oil needed will depend on the person. 1-2 tablespoons can be used in the evening, or in the morning before consuming any food. Follow with one cup of warm water. If one tablespoon does not work after three nights, increase to two tablespoons.

**Psyllium Husks/Powder:** Psyllium is a bulk fiber which can have a laxative effect when taken in the correct way. Psyllium is a mucolodge, and helps to promote the correct environment in the intestinal tract. It will help to scrape toxins from the GI tract. Psyllium is heavy, meaning that it can get stuck in some people's GI tract. To prevent this it can be taken with ½ tsp of dry ginger powder, which is light and dry and helps to promote movement in the intestinal tract. Take one tablespoon of psyllium with ½ teaspoon of dry ginger before dinner or lunch. Give the psyllium 20 minutes to digest before consuming lunch.

**Flax seeds:** As a laxative Flaxseeds can be infused in water and drunk each night before sleep. For use as a bulk laxative one tablespoon can be ground and taken as a powder twice per day (morning and evening). As a general digestive the crushed seeds can be infused in water over night and drunk cold the next morning before breakfast. Flax Seed oil is also good for constipation, take one tablespoon before bedtime.

## Regulating Apana Vayu with Water

This is a remedy for regulating Apana vayu, which is most effective for Vata and Pitta types of constitution. It will be much less effective for kapha types who already have much water in the body already.

Before sunrise (will not work after sunrise), drink 1 liter of warm to hot water. This lubricates the body, and helps apana vayu to be regulated at the end of the Vata period (3-6am). It may take a few days to take effect. This should be continued for 30 days.

## Enemas and Colonics

Enemas and colonics are a method of cleaning out the colon. Enemas will clean out the bottom portion of the rectum, while colonics clean out the entire colon. They are temporary solutions, which provide relief because the fecal matter is cleaned out. It is important that they are done in the correct method, and followed up with the correct therapies. Cleaning the colon with an excess of plain water can dry out the colon, and increase constipation due to dryness after the colonic or enema. In addition, frequent colonics or enemas can disrupt apana vayu, because they promote movement in the opposite direction than is normal for apana vayu. While it is fine to use them for temporary relief of constipation, be aware of developing a dependency on enemas to have a bowel movement. It is very important to follow a cleansing enema with an oil enema.

***All preceding articles have been contributed by Paul Dallaghan and Jessica Blanchard.***

Beachfront lounge at Samahita Retreat

# The Core Ingredients

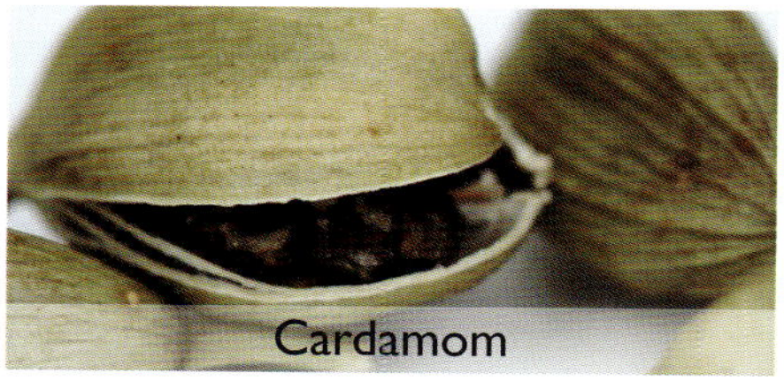

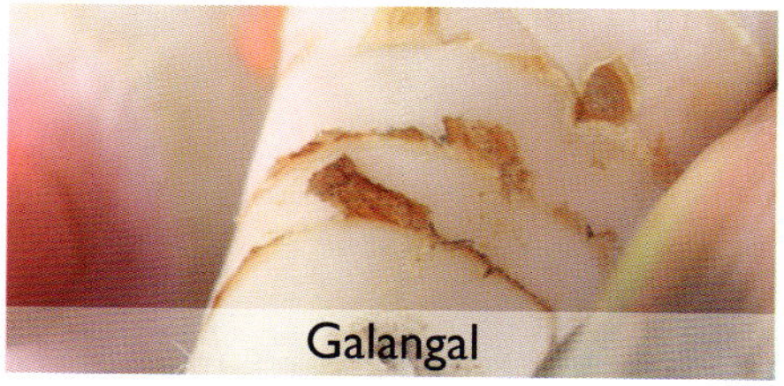


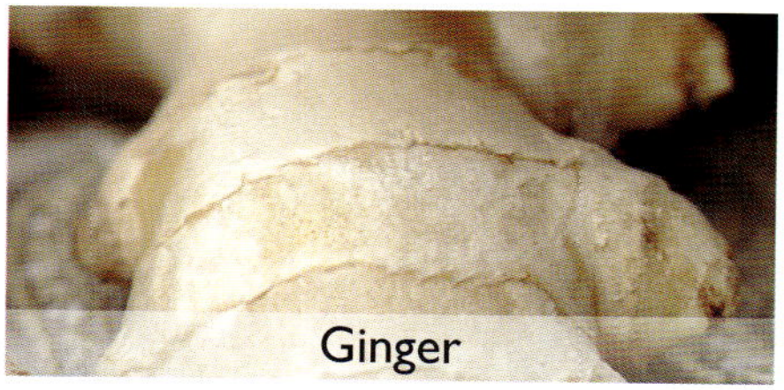

# Essentials from India

## Ghee

**Ingredients:**
1 pack unsalted butter (organic)

**Instructions:**
Heat the butter on medium heat until it boils. Then turn down the heat, and let cook around 20 minutes. Watch the butter carefully. The milk solids will start to settle on the bottom of the pan and the ghee will also turn a golden color. When boiling, it will make a crackling sound. When the crackling sound stops, the ghee is about done. Cook around another 2 minutes, until the color deepens. Remove from heat, strain out the milk solids that have settled on the bottom of the pan. Store the ghee in clean glass jars at room temperature (not in the refrigerator). Ghee can keep for several months.

# Chapatis

Unleavened flatbread. The spices are optional and can be used for variety.

## Ingredients:

2 cups whole wheat flour
½ tsp each cumin seeds, mineral salt (optional)
¼ tsp each ground cumin, coriander, turmeric (optional)
Water

## Instructions:

Mix the flour, spices and salt. Slowly add water while mixing the dough until the dough becomes moist. Kneed until smooth. It is good to let the dough rest around 20 minutes, but not necessary. Take some dough about the size of a golf ball and roll out until very thin. Use extra flour on both sides of the dough to keep the chapati from sticking to the roller or the surface. Cook the chapati on cast iron pan over medium-high heat, around 1 minute on each side. The chapati should brown in spots as bubbles form and make it rise slightly. You can press the chappati with a spatula, and flip it a few times, to help it to cook evenly without burning. Optionally, you can put it on a gas flame on each side to make it puff up.

# Caffeine-Free Chai

Chai is traditionally made with black tea, but the hebs and spices can be enjoyed with this caffeine-free version.

**Ingredients:**

½ cup chopped fresh ginger
1 tsp peppercorns
6 star anise
1 tsp cloves
5 cardamom pods (crushed and seeded)
5-7 cinnamon sticks
4 cups of water

**Instructions:**

Put ingredients in saucepan with water, bring to boil. Keep adding water as the water boils out. Add more cinnamon to increase sweetness. Boil 5-10 minutes stirring occasionally. Drain, let cool, and put into glass container.

**Serving suggestions:**

For the traditional method, add black tea with milk, heat to boiling. Sweeten as desired with brown sugar or honey. This recipe makes 1 pot (4 cups)

# Milk Rice

This is a very sattvic dinner, that is also very satisfying. It is best with basmati rice, which is very easy to digest, but can be made with brown rice, or with white rice. If making with brown rice, it is best to soak the rice for at least 4 hours beforehand.

**Ingredients:**
Serves one person:
1½ cups whole milk (you may need more, depending on desired consistency)
ghee
¼ cup of brown/white rice or one handful of rice
Brown sugar to taste

**Optional:**
1 tbsp raisins, soaked in water for one hour to remove acidity
1 cardamom pod, opened with the seeds crushed

**Instructions:**
Heat the ghee in a pot. Add the rice and fry for one minute. Add the milk and boil until the rice is cooked. For brown rice this takes around 40 minutes, for white rice, around 20 minutes. Add sugar to taste.

# How to Make a Vegetarian Thai Curry Paste?

Thai curry paste is the main ingredient in almost any Thai curries, soups or sauces. If you have an Asian grocery store, these pastes are available in a ready made jar or can. However most of the ready made products are not vegetarian and contain shrimp or fish sauce. We have created a quick and simple way to make your own vegetarian curry paste with a mortal and pestle or a food processor. It takes no time as long as you have the ingredients. You can also store the paste in a fridge and can keep it for a long time.

# Green Curry Paste

**Ingredients:**

15 small green chili
3 large bell pepper
½ tsp sea salt
5 black pepper corns
1 tbsp finely chopped galangal
2 tbsp finely chopped lemongrass
1 tsp minced bergamot leaves
1 tsp chopped coriander root
¼ cup peeled garlic cloves
7 chopped red onions
1 tbsp vegetarian shrimp paste, soybean paste or miso paste

**Instructions:**

Blend together green chili, sea salt and black peppers. Add finely chopped galangal, lemongrass, minced bergamot leaves, coriander root and peeled garlic cloves. Mix together until the paste is even. Then, add chopped red onions and vegetarian shrimp paste or soy paste. Blend the mixture together until it is smooth texture.

# Massaman Curry Paste

**Ingredients:**

5 large sundried red chili
1 tsp sea salt
1 tbsp finely chopped roasted galangal
1 tablespoon finely chopped roasted lemongrass
2 grilled garlic cloves
5 grilled red onions
1 tsp grind pepper
1 tbsp roasted ground coriander
1 tsp roasted ground cumin
2 cloves
1 tsp vegetarian shrimp paste, soybean paste or miso paste

**Instructions:**

Take out the chili seeds and put chili in water until skin is smooth. Blend together dried chili and sea salt. Add galangal, lemongrass, garlic cloves and red onions into mixtures. Then, add ground pepper, coriander, cloves and vegetarian shrimp paste or soy paste. Mix together until the paste is even.

# Yellow Curry Paste

**Ingredients:**

5 large sundried red chili
1 tsp sea salt
1 tsp finely chopped galangal
1 tbsp finely chopped lemongrass
1 tsp finely chopped bergamot skin
2 tsp chopped coriander root
5 black pepper corn
10 peeled garlic cloves
5 chopped red onions
1 tsp roasted ground cumin
1 tsp vegetarian shrimp paste, soy paste or miso paste

**Instructions:**

Take out the chili seeds and put chili in water until skin is smooth. Blend together dried chili and sea salt. Add galangal, lemongrass, chopped bergamot skin, coriander root, black peppers and garlic cloves into the mixtures. When smooth, put together red onions, coriander root, cumin and vegetarian shrimp paste or soy paste. Mix together until paste is even.

# Thai Curries

We make delicious vegetarian versions of Thailand's famous curry soups, "ghang". We give basic cooking guidelines, however, you can vary the amounts of ingredients, especially the curry pastes, according to your taste. Most curry paste that you buy "off the shelf" may contains fish sauce and shrimp paste and often are too spicy. If the curry paste is too spicy, you can lower the quantity of the paste but add more Thai herbs like lemongrass, galangal and basil leaves to give it more flavor.

*Green Curry*

# Green Curry

**Ingredients:**

2 cups chopped vegetables, can include any of the following: broccoli, cauliflower, green beans, pumpkin, baby corn, carrots, winter melon
1 tbsp green curry paste
3 cups coconut milk
1 tbsp veggie soup stock powder
Salt to taste
1 handful of fresh basil
1 tbsp brown sugar

**Instructions:**

Combine all ingredients except the basil in a large pot. Cook for 20 minutes. Sprinkle with the basil and serve with brown rice.

Serves 2

# Penang Coconut Curry

This is another delicious curry, which is similar in taste to the green curry and has bit more of the curry flavor.

**Ingredients:**

2 cups of chopped vegetables, can include any of the following: broccoli, cauliflower, green beans, pumpkin, baby corn, carrots, winter melon
½ tbsp yellow curry paste
½ tbsp massaman curry paste
3 cups coconut milk
1 tsp turmeric
1 tbsp veggie soup stock powder
Salt to taste
1 handful of fresh basil
1 tbsp brown sugar

**Instructions:**

Combine all ingredients except the basil in a large pot. Cook for 20-30 minutes. Sprinkle with the basil and serve with brown rice.

Serves 2

# Massaman Curry

This delicious curry is a favorite for a hearty lunch. The tamarinds and brown sugar give it a delicious sweet and sour flavor.

**Ingredients:**

1 ½ cups peeled and chopped potatoes
1 cup peeled and chopped carrots
4 cups coconut milk
½ cup peanuts
1 cup tamarinds, soaked in 1 cup of boiling water
1 tbsp red curry paste
¼ cup brown sugar
Pinch of salt

**Instructions:**

Sauté the red curry paste with a little coconut milk in a large pot. Add the rest of the coconut milk, the carrots and potatoes, bring the mixture to a boil. Mix the tamarinds in water, to break up the bits of fruit. Strain the tamarind juice into the boiling curry. Let the curry boil for 45 minutes. Add the peanuts. Serve with brown rice.

Serves 2

# "Kanom Jeen" Thai Yellow Curry with Rice Noodles

This is a newer addition to our menu, which has become one of our favorites. As a nice change, it is served with rice noodles rather than brown rice.

**Ingredients:**
2 firm tofu (16 oz)
4 cups coconut milk
1 tbsp yellow curry paste
2 lime leaves, cut very thinly
Pinch of salt
1 package of thin rice noodles

**Instructions:**
Sauté the red curry paste with a little coconut milk in a large pot. Crumble up tofu so that it is a fine consistency. Add the rest of the coconut milk and the tofu to the curry paste, bring to a boil. Add a bit of salt. Boil the curry for 10-15 minutes, until the curry is a thicker consistency. Add the lime leaves when it is done cooking.

Boil water for the rice noodles and cook the rice noodles until tender. Serve and enjoy!

Serves 2

# "Gaeng The-Pho" Thai Tamarind Curry with Morning Glory

**Ingredients:**
6 cups morning glory or mustard greens
4 cups coconut milk
1 tsp yellow curry paste
¼ cup of tamarind paste
2-3 kaffir lime leaves, cut thinly
Pinch of salt
Brown rice

**Instructions:**
Put the tamarind seeds in hot water, let soak for 5 minutes and strain out the juice. If you are using the paste, simply mix it with ½ cup of hot water. Sauté the yellow curry paste with a little coconut milk in a large pot. Add the tamarind juice to the coconut milk. Add the rest of the coconut milk and the tofu to the curry paste, bring to a boil. Add a bit of salt. Add the morning glory to the coconut milk mixture. Boil the curry for 20 minutes, until the vegetables are cooked. Add the lime leaves when it is done cooking.

Serves 2

# Tofu Dishes

We use locally homemade tofu made daily here on Koh Samui. The fresh tofu makes the food very tasteful and easy to digest as its not processed. We recommend you use extra firm tofu for these recipes.

*"Haw Muk" Steamed Tofu in Banana Leaves*

# "Haw Mok" Steam Tofu in Banana Leaves

This dish is normally made with seafood of some type, however, we love the tofu version. The coconut milk gives the tofu a delicious flavor, and the banana leaves make it an aesthetically pleasing dish.

**Ingredients:**

2 firm tofu (16 oz)
2 cups coconut milk (the amount may vary, based on the texture of the tofu)
½ cup shredded cabbage and carrot
½-1 tsp of salt
1 tsp powdered veggie soup stock powder
1/3 tsp white pepper
4-5 lime leaves
1 tsp yellow curry paste
1 tbsp brown sugar
Handful of fresh basil leaves
Banana leaves for serving or small ceramic dishes

**Instructions:**

Break up the tofu until it is crumbly. Mix the salt, veggie soup stock, curry paste, pepper, and coconut milk together in a separate bowl. Stir into the tofu, mix vigorously for 10 minutes until the coconut milk mixture is well infused into the tofu. Add the carrots and cabbage and again mix together. We use banana leaves to make small dishes for serving the tofu or fish. Coat the bottom of the dish or banana leaves with basil. Spoon the mixture into the banana leaves, steam in a large pot for 15 minutes.

Serves 4

# "Laab" Tofu

One of the Samahita Retreat favorites, this is a vegetarian version of a traditional Thai dish typically made with chicken. The amount of spices can be adjusted depending on how spicy you like it. It can be served with green salad as a light appetizer.

**Ingredients:**

2 firm tofu (16 oz)
1 tbsp oil
2 stalks of lemongrass
1 cucumber
3 red chilies
4 tbsp lemon juice
Handful of fresh coriander and mint leaves
Salt to taste
½ cup pan-roasted rice (which we buy already roasted and crushed, you can substitute crushed sesame seeds)

**Instructions:**

Heat the oil in a saucepan, fry the tofu for 10 minutes on each side, until it is lightly brown. Alternatively, the tofu can be cooked in the oven, by wrapping it in foil, and baking for 20 minutes. After cooking, dry on paper towels and let cool. Mash up the tofu so that it is crumbly. Chop up the lemongrass, cucumber, chilies, mint leaves and coriander. Add to the tofu along with the lemon juice, pan roasted rice and salt. Mix together and serve.

Serves 2

# Coconut Curry Tofu

Tofu can be substituted for fish, shrimp or squid, in which case, less salt will be needed. For a spicier version, double the amount of red curry paste.

**Ingredients:**

2 firm tofu (16 oz)
3-4 cups coconut milk (less coconut milk for a thicker, more seasoned sauce)
½-1 tsp of salt
1 tsp veggie soup stock powder
1/3 tsp white pepper
4-5 lime leaves
1 tsp red curry paste
1 tbsp oil

**Instructions:**

Heat oil for frying in large wok or frying pan. Fry the tofu patties for 5-10 minutes, turning once. The outside of the tofu should be golden brown. Drain the tofu, chop into small bite size chunks. Lightly salt and set aside.

Heat the coconut milk it a wok or large saucepan. Add the salt, veggie soup stock or dried mushroom soup stock, white pepper and red curry paste. When the coconut milk comes to a boil, add the tofu. Cook on medium heat for 15-20 minutes, until the coconut milk slightly thickens.

Serves 2

# Ginger Malay Tofu

This dish from Malaysia is another simple yet tasty way to prepare tofu. The ginger sauce goes nicely with some ghee and brown rice.

**Ingredients:**
¼ cup chopped ginger (into small matchstick sized strips)
2 firm tofu (16 oz)
2 tbsp soy sauce
2 tbsp black soy sauce (or soy mixed with molasses)
2 tbsp veggie soup stock powder
½ tsp white pepper
2 cups water
1 tbsp oil
½ cup coarsely chopped coriander
Chopped kaffir leaves

**Instructions:**
Heat oil for frying in large wok or frying pan. Fry the tofu patties for 5-10 minutes, turning once. The outside of the tofu should be golden brown. Drain and chop into small bite size chunks. Lightly salt and set aside.

Heat 2 tbsp of oil in wok. Add ginger and stir fry around 5 minutes. Drain the oil. Add the soy, veggie soup stock powder, white pepper and water to the wok. Bring to boil. Simmer 20 minutes, until the sauce thickens. Stir occasionally to keep the ginger from sticking to the pan. Add the tofu and coriander and heat through. Serve garnished with the lime leaves.

Serves 2

# Spicy Curry Tofu

This is a simple and tasty way to prepare tofu. It goes well with the slightly sweet taste of the Mee Gorang Noodles.

**Ingredients:**
2 firm tofu (16 oz)
2 cups chopped green beans
1-2 tsp red curry paste
3-4 tbsp soy sauce
1 tbsp oil
5 kaffir lime leaves chopped

**Instructions:**
Heat oil for frying in large wok or frying pan. Deep fry tofu patties for 5-10 minutes, turning once. The outside of the tofu should be golden brown. Drain the tofu, chop into small bite size chunks. Lightly salt and set aside.

Heat 2 tbsp oil in wok or frying pan. Add the curry paste and stir. Add the green beans and cook, stirring occasionally for 10 minutes. Add the tofu and soy sauce, stir well and cook another 5 minutes. Sprinkle with chopped lime leaves and serve!

Serves 2

# Sweet and Sour Tofu

**Ingredients:**
2 firm tofu (16 oz)
3 cups chopped vegetables: baby corn, red pepper, green pepper, carrots, cucumber
2 tbsp tomato ketchup
1 tbsp white vinegar
3-4 tbsp soy sauce
1 tbsp veggie soup stock powder
1 tbsp oil
½ cup fresh coriander, leaves and the stalks
2 cups chopped pineapple

**Instructions:**
Heat oil for frying in large wok or frying pan. Deep fry tofu patties for 5-10 minutes, turning once. The outside of the tofu should be golden brown. Drain the tofu, chop into small bite size chunks. Lightly salt and set aside.

Or in the oven:
Wrap the tofu in aluminum foil. Bake in a medium heat oven for around 20 minutes, until the tofu is firm and seems cooked.

Heat oil in wok or frying pan, add the vegetables, and stir well. Add all the seasoning ingredients except the coriander. Stir well. Cook for 10 minutes. Add the cooked fish or tofu to the vegetables, add the fresh coriander, and cook for 5 additional minutes.

Serves 2

# Tofu Burger

**Ingredients:**
1 firm tofu (8 oz)
Finely chopped coriander
Finely chopped tomatoes
1 tbsp white sesame
1 tbsp soy sauce
1 tbsp cumin powder
½ tbsp veggie soup stock powder
Whole wheat bun
Sauce (ketchup or mayonnaise)
1 tsp oil

**Instructions:**
Crush tofu by hand into small pieces. Add in other ingredients and mix together until smooth. Make the mixture into round flat shape, not too thick. Heat the oil and fry the tofu burger for 10 – 15 minutes or until brown. Put aside and let cool. It can make up to 4 servings.

Cut whole wheat bun in half. Add tofu burger, sliced cucumber, tomato and green vegetable. Serve with ketchup or mayonnaise.

Serves 1

# Soups

We often serve the "lighter" soups at night to help nurture us after a long day of practice, and won't leave us feeling too full for early morning practice.

*"Tom Kha" Coconut Lemongrass Soup*

# "Tom Kha" Coconut Lemongrass Soup

**Ingredients:**

3 cups chopped vegetables:
carrots, baby corn, green beans, cauliflower, pumpkin, winter melon
5 cups of coconut milk
3 stalks of lemongrass chopped
5 lime leaves
1 large chunk of galangal chopped in large pieces, around ¼ cup (a root seasoning which resembles ginger)
½ tbsp salt
½ tbsp white pepper
¼ cap of lime juice

**Instructions:**

Combine all ingredients except the lime juice in a large pot. Bring to boil and cook 20 minutes, stirring occasionally. The stirring will keep the coconut from separating from the water. Add the lime juice and cook another 5 minutes.

Serves 3

# Minestrone Soup

**Ingredients:**

1 cup cabbage
1 cup green beans
1 cup baby corn
1 cup carrot
1 cup bell pepper
1 cup potato
2 cups water
1 tbsp tomato paste
1 cup canned tomato juice
1 tbsp oregano, thyme
½ tbsp black pepper
1 tbsp salt
1 tbsp olive oil
1 tsp brown sugar
Add pasta (optional)

**Instructions:**

All vegetables cut in small square cube. Heat olive oil until warm, add potato and water. Add seasoning. When the potato is cooked, add remaining vegetables. Then add tomato paste and juice. Wait until vegetables are cooked then add oregano and thyme. Cook for about 20 minutes.

Serves 2

# Winter Melon Vegetable Soup

**Ingredients:**

2 cups winter melon (or similar type vegetable)
1 cup baby corn
½ cup carrot
2 crushed root of cilantro root
1 tsp salt
½ tsp black pepper
1 tsp soy sauce
¼ cilantro leafs chopped
1 cup soft tofu
2 cups water

**Instructions:**

Boil water with cilantro root and black pepper. Cut winter melon into 2 inch square. Cut carrot and baby corn into smaller pieces. Wait until water boils and then add salt, soy sauce, all vegetables and soft tofu. Cook for 15 minutes.

Serves 2

# "Tom Yum" Vegetable Soup

The lemongrass, galangal, and lemon juice give this soup a wonderful flavor.

**Ingredients:**

3 cups chopped vegetables: carrots, fresh baby corn, green beans, pumpkin, winter melon, cabbage
3 lemon grass stalks, chopped coarsely
½ cup galangal sliced
10 kaffir lime leaves
Juice of 3 lemons or limes
1 tbsp veggie soup stock powder
2 green chilies chopped (optional)
1 tsp vegetarian chili paste
White pepper to taste
Salt to taste
2 cups water

**Instructions:**

Combine all the ingredients except the lemon juice. Bring to a boil and cook for 30 minutes. Turn off the heat, add the lemon juice and stir well.

Serves 2

# Pumpkin Soup

Our fresh vegetable soups are very popular. They are perfect for a light meal, and go well with a salad or a little brown rice.

**Ingredients:**
8 cups pumpkin sliced
6 cups water
1 tsp salt
½ tsp white pepper
2 tbsp chopped ginger
2 tbsp veggie soup stock powder
Chopped coriander

**Instructions:**
Cook pumpkin in salted water until soft, drain and set the water used for cooking aside. Put the vegetables into a blender, and blend until they are broken up. Return to the saucepan, add the ginger and water. Stir, add water until the soup reaches the desired consistency. Add pepper and soup stock. Cook for 10 minutes. Add the coriander for garnish and serve.

Serves 4

# "Rassam" Indian Tomato Soup

This is a very fragrant, light soup that is only found in south India. Its flavor comes from Rassam powder, a mix of spices that can be bought already mixed.

**Ingredients:**
1 cup tuur dahl
4 cups tomatoes
2-3 tbsp coriander leaves
10 curry leaves
2 tbsp grated coconut
1 tsp of MTR Rassam powder, or MDH Rassam powder (bought at indian food store)
1 tbsp jaggery or brown sugar
1 tsp tamarind juice (soak tamarinds in boiling water, take the juice)
6 cups water

**Instructions:**
Cook the lentils and tomatoes in the water until the lentils are very soft, (will take around 30 minutes). Remove the tomatoes and mash or put in the blender to break them up. Add the salt, jaggery, Rassam powder, curry leaves, coriander, and tamarind juice. Cook until the mixture boils. Add the grated coconut and the garnish.

**For the garnish:**
2 tsp ghee
½ tsp mustard seeds
2 pinches of asafetida
½ tsp cumin seeds

Heat the ghee, add the mustard seeds. When they begin to pop, add the other ingredients. Cook 2 minutes, set aside.

Serves 2

# Indian Mixed Vegetable Soup

**Ingredients**

4 cups of assorted vegetables in season, for example: cauliflower, carrots, cabbage, peas, green beans, winter melon (or another type of squash), potatoes, tomatoes
Fresh ginger
1 tbsp coriander powder
1 tbsp cumin powder
1 tsp black pepper
1 tsp salt
Juice of 1 lemon
1 tbsp ghee

**Instructions:**

Boil the vegetables in around 6 cups of water for 20 minutes, until they are tender. Let the vegetables and water cool somewhat. Puree the vegetables and water in the blender. Return to the pan. Heat ghee in a separate small pan, add fresh ginger, black pepper, and coriander powder. Fry cumin powder in pan separately. Add spices to the vegetables. Add lemon juice.

Serves 3

# Bean & Lentil Recipes

Dahl, which is the Indian word for lentil, is an essential part of a healthy vegetarian diet. The most important types of dahl are mung dahl, small yellow lentils which are used in so many popular Indian dishes. They are the split form of the mung bean, which is green and one of the easiest beans to sprout. Sprouted mung beans and mung dahl are some of the easiest forms of protein to digest. Here are a few of our favorite recipes.

*Sprouted Mung Falafel with Yoghurt Sauce*

# Sprouted Mung Falafel with Yoghurt Sauce

This is a more easily digestable version of the classic chick pea falafel (which is acidic and aggravating to Pitta dosha), we also like to bake it rather than fry it, to keep it light.

**Ingredients:**
3 cups sprouted mung beans (if you don't use sprouted, soak the mung overnight).
2 tbsp cumin powder
2 tbsp coriander powder
3 tbsp chopped ginger
1 tsp black pepper (adjust to taste)
2 tsp salt (adjust to taste)
½ cup chopped fresh coriander
¼ cup chopped fresh mint
2 tbsp olive oil + olive oil for drizzling before baking
1 cup bread crumbs

**Instructions:**
Cook the mung beans in boiling water for 30 minutes, until they are soft. They can also be cooked in a pressure cooker for 15 minutes. Drain the mung beans, and let cool enough to handle them. Add the cumin, coriander, ginger, black pepper, salt and olive oil. Mix well with a big spoon, until the mung is slightly mashed and all the spices are well integrated with the mung. Form the paste into small balls, around 1.5 inches or 4 cm in diameter, roll in bread crumbs, then place into a baking pan. Drizzle with olive oil and a little sea salt and black pepper. Bake for 20 minutes at 375 degrees F until the outside is slightly crisp. Serve with yoghurt sauce, grilled veggies and chapatis.

## Yoghurt Sauce:

**Ingredients:**
2 cups plain, full-fat yoghurt
¼ cup fresh mint
¼ cup fresh coriander
1 tbsp lemon juice
Dash of soy sauce or Bragg's Amino Acids
Salt and black pepper to taste
Mix all the ingredients together and serve!

Serves 6 pieces

# Kitcheri

"Kitcheri" literally means, "cooked with rice and mung dahl." In South India it is known as Pongal. This is a classic Indian dish, that can be made many ways with larger proportions of mung beans, with additional vegetables, fewer spices, it is up to you. For a soupier result, increase the amount of water. Kitcheri is very nourishing, yet easily digested; it is strengthening and easy for your body to use, which means its great for illness recovery. Kitcheri is the main diet in our yogi's detox program.

**Ingredients:**
1 tbsp ghee
2 tbsp 2-3 ginger (depending on how you like ginger)
Pinch of asafetida
1 tsp cumin seeds
1 tsp ground cumin
1-2 tsp salt
1 tsp turmeric powder
¾ cup chopped carrots and potatoes
1 cup rice
1 cup mung beans
4-6 cups water (the amount of water depends on the type of rice used, and how soupy you like the Kitcheri)
10 curry leaves (optional)

**Instructions:**
Rinse the rice and mung beans until the water becomes clear. If you have time, soak the rice and mung together for an hour or two. Heat the ghee in a saucepan, add the curry leaves and half the ginger, then stir. Add the asafetida, cumin seeds, cumin powder and stir. Add the salt and turmeric, stir. Add the rice/mung mixture, stirring rapidly, so that the bottom of the pan doesn't burn. Cook 1-2 minutes in the ghee, then add the water, carrots and potatoes, and the remaining ginger. Bring to a boil, then cover. Cook 15-20 minutes, until the water is absorbed.

Serves 3

# Sprouted Mung Beans

Mung beans are much easier to digest, and have more 'prana' or life force, when they are sprouted.

**Ingredients:**
2 cups whole mung beans
Water
Large flat pan

**Instructions:**
Rinse the mung beans well. In drier cooler climates, it is necessary to soak the mung beans in water overnight. In Thailand, we don't have to do this, we can simply wet them, put them into a flat pan, and they sprout. Once soaked, put them into a flat pan, they need to stay moist. You should rinse them a few times a day, and keep them covered with a damp towel. Keeping them in a darker place helps. You will see that small sprouts start to appear, when they are 1 cm or ½ inch long. Rinse them again, put into an airtight container into the refrigerator.

Yield 2 cups

# South-Indian Mung Beans

A simple recipe that was served to some of us by Swami Bramhananda, in B.R. Hills, outside of Mysore.

**Ingredients:**

3 cups sprouted mung beans, or soaked overnight
2 tbsp chopped ginger
1 tbsp ghee
1 tsp mustard seeds
1 tbsp cumin powder
Pinch of asafetida
1 handful of grated coconut
1 handful of fresh coriander
Salt and black pepper to taste

**Instructions:**

Cook the mung beans in boiling water for 30 minutes, until tender, then drain. Heat the ghee in a skillet, add the mustard seeds, when they begin to pop add the asafetida, cumin powder, and fresh ginger. Saute for 1-2 minutes, then add the mung beans to the ghee and spice mixture, stir well. Add salt and black pepper to taste. Garnish with coconut and coriander.

Serves 2

# Yellow Mung Dahl Soup

**Ingredients:**

1 cup yellow mung dal
6 cups water
1 tsp ghee
¼ tsp each black mustard seeds, ground cumin, ground coriander, turmeric
1 tsp cumin seeds
1 pinch asafoetida
½ tsp mineral or Sea salt
¼ cup fresh coriander or cilantro leaves, chopped

**Instructions:**

Wash the dal until the water runs clear. Cook the dal in water for 30 minutes, until soft (10-15 minutes in pressure cooker). In a small saucepan, cook the mustard seeds in ghee over medium heat until the seeds begin to pop. Remove from heat and add the rest of the spices and stir. When dal is cooked, add the spice mixture and salt or Bragg's Liquid Amino's to taste. Garnish with cilantro or coriander.

Serves 2

# Vegetarian Chili

This is a nice recipe that is not too spicy, but very flavorful.

**Ingredients:**

2 cups dry red kidney beans (soak overnight)
1 cup textured soy protein (soaked for a 2 hours)
Approximately 6 cups of water (enough for cooking beans generously in water)
1-2 tsp olive oil
1 carrot
4 small tomatoes (or 2 large)
1 each of green pepper, yellow pepper, and red pepper
2 tsp cumin powder
Salt to taste
Pepper to taste
1 tsp rosemary
1 tsp thyme
2 tbsp tomato paste
1 can of tomato juice

**Instructions:**

Place the kidney beans in a large pot with the water. Cover and boil until tender. This may take 1 to 2 hours. Add the soy protein when the beans have finished cooking.

Heat the oil in a skillet. Add the carrot, peppers, salt, cumin, rosemary and thyme. Sauté over medium heat until the carrot and peppers are tender, around 15 minutes. Add this mixture to the beans.

Add the tomato paste and tomato juice to the mixture. Add salt and pepper to taste. Simmer over very low heat for an additional 10 minutes. At the end, add a handful of basil and cilantro.

Serves 4

# Indian Red Bean Soup

**Ingredients:**

2 cups red beans
2 tbsp grated or finely chopped fresh ginger
Pinch of asafetida
2 bay leaves
1 tbsp coriander powder
3 finely chopped tomatoes
1 tbsp ghee
1 tsp salt
½ cup fresh coriander
1 or 2 green chilis

**Instructions:**

Soak the beans overnight. Cook the beans in around 6 cups of water for one hour, until they are soft. Heat the ghee in a large pot. Add the asafetida, ginger, and coriander powder. Stir well. After 1-2 minutes, add the tomatoes, chilis, and salt. Stir well. Cook for 5 minutes, until the tomatoes are soft. Then add the beans, and their water to the tomatoes. You may remove some of the water if you would prefer a thicker soup. Just before serving, add fresh coriander.

Serves 2

# Brazilian Black Bean Soup

This is a delicious soup, an explosion of flavors that will please even the pickiest of palates. We've "yogified" it from the recipe in the fantastic vegetarian classic, the Moosewood Cookbook by Mollie Katzken.

As a preliminary preparation, soak the black beans overnight or at least for four hours.

**Ingredients:**
2 cups dry black beans
6 cups water
Pinch of asafetida (not mandatory, but helps to remove gas)
1-2 tbsp olive oil
1 chopped onion
2 tsp cumin
2 tsp salt
1 carrot, diced
1 green pepper, diced
1 ½ cups fresh orange juice
Black pepper
Handful of cilantro
1 lime

**Instructions:**
Place the black beans in a large pot with the water. Add the asafetida. Cover and boil until tender. In Thailand this takes at least 2 hours. In the west, it should take around 1 ¼ hours.

Heat the oil in a skillet. Add the onion, cumin, salt, and carrot. Sauté over medium heat until the carrot is tender and the onion is caramelized. Add the green pepper. Sauté until everything is very tender, around 10 or 15 minutes. Add the mixture to the beans.

Stir the orange juice and black pepper into the beans. Puree the soup in a blender or food processor and return to the pot. Simmer over a very low heat for an additional 10 minutes. Add a handful of cilantro and a squeeze of lime before serving.

Serves 2

**Notes:**

# Noodles

*"Pad"* means to fry over flame, so all these dishes are stir fry. It's best to use a wok. Most Thai noodle dishes are made from white rice noodles. You should always soak the noodles in room temperature water first before use.

*Glass Noodle Stir fry*

# Glass Noodle Stir Fry

**Ingredients:**
16 oz thin glass noodles
1 cup shredded cabbage
1 cup bean sprouts
1 cup shredded carrots
2 tbsp oil
Water for cooking noodles
1 tbsp veggie soup stock powder
2-4 tbsp soy sauce
½ tsp black pepper

**Instructions:**
Heat water to boiling in large wok or saucepan. Cook the noodles just until tender, then drain and set aside. Heat oil in wok, add the shredded vegetables, soy sauce, veggie soup stock powder and black pepper. Stir rapidly and continue to sauté for 2-3 minutes. Add the noodles, stir in the seasonings and vegetables, sauté for another 2-3 minutes until warm.

Serves 4

# Pad Thai

**Ingredients:**

16 oz medium rice noodles
½ cup cabbage
1 cup bean sprouts
2 tbsp white vinegar
4-6 tbsp black soy sauce
2-3 tbsp soy sauce
1 tbsp brown sugar
2 eggs (optional)
2 tbsp oil
1 tbsp veggie soup stock powder
soup stock
1 tsp black pepper
½ cup peanuts

**Instructions:**

Boil the noodles in salted water until tender, around 5-7 minutes. Drain in cool water and set aside. To prepare the peanuts, heat a pan or wok, put the peanuts on the heated wok. Cook for 5 minutes, remove from heat and let cool. Chop when cooled. Heat oil in wok or frying pan, add cabbage, and half the sprouts. Stir fry for 5 minutes. Add eggs, noodles, vinegar, soy sauce, black soy sauce, veggie soup stock powder and stir together in wok. Cook for another 5 minutes. Just before serving, add the peanuts and the remaining sprouts, stir to distribute. The amounts of soy sauce, sugar, pepper can be adjusted to taste.

Serves 4

# Pad See Eiw

This delicious dish is always a favorite at lunchtime. The black soy sauce gives it a dark color, and a rich flavor. If you cannot find black soy sauce, use regular soy sauce, mixed with a bit of molasses.

**Ingredients:**
16 oz wide rice noodles
2 cups chopped thick, leafy greens such as kale
2 tbsp white vinegar
4-6 tbsp black soy sauce
2-3 tbsp soy sauce
1 tbsp brown sugar
2 tbsp oil
1 tbsp veggie soup stock
1 tsp black pepper
1 cup bean sprouts

**Instructions:**
Boil the noodles in salted water until tender, around 5-7 minutes. Drain in cool water and set aside. To prepare the peanuts, heat a pan or wok, put the peanuts on the heated wok. Cook for 5 minutes, remove from heat and let cool. Chop when cooled. Heat oil in wok or frying pan, add cabbage and half the sprouts stir fry for 5 minutes. Add eggs, noodles, vinegar, soy sauce, black soy sauce, veggie soup stock powder and stir together in wok. Cook another 5 minutes. Just before serving, add the peanuts and the remaining sprouts, stir to distribute. The amounts of soy sauce, sugar, pepper can be adjusted to taste.

Serves 4

# Mee Gorang Noodles

This is a famous Indonesian dish. As an option, it can be made with eggs.

**Ingredients:**

16 oz dry noodles (like ramen noodles)
2-4 tbsp soy sauce
2 cups shredded cabbage and carrots
2 tbsp oil
2 tbsp veggie soup stock powder
1 tsp white pepper
2 tbsp white vinegar
1 cup coarsely chopped coriander

**Instructions:**

Cook noodles in salt and hot water and set aside. Heat oil in wok or frying pan and add cabbage and carrots. Cook for 3-5 minutes, until vegetables are just tender. Add noodles and the other ingredients, stirring vigorously. Cook another 3 minutes. If using eggs, mix 2-3 with soy sauce, and cook until still runny in another pan. Then add to the noodles at the end of the cooking.

Serves 4

# Sattvic Pesto Pasta

Su makes a delicious version of this Italian favorite, which is unique in that we don't use any onion or garlic to make the sauce.

**Ingredients:**
3 bunches of fresh basil (around 1 ½ cups of fresh basil)
¼ cup extra virgin olive oil
6 cashew nuts
Salt to taste
1 lb of pasta
Grated parmesan cheese

**Instructions:**
Cook the pasta in salted water.
Put the basil, olive oil and salt in a blender or use a mortar and pestle to mash the basil and olive oil together. Crush the cashews separately and add to the pesto mixture. Add salt to taste. Add the pesto sauce to cooked pasta and serve.

Serves 4

# Rice

We use brown rice when possible for all our of our dishes. For convenience and ease, we recommend using an electric rice cooker. Just add more water and time for brown rice. For Indian dishes, you can use white basmati rice depending on your cooking method.

*Vegetarian Sushi*

# Vegetarian Sushi

This has been a recent addition to our menu, and is a big hit with the guests. It is nice to get the different flavors of wasabi and seaweed.

**Ingredients:**
2 cups of cooked brown rice
1 tbsp brown sugar
2 tbsp rice vinegar
Assorted cooked vegetables: pumpkin, carrot, green beans, they can be cooked in soya sauce or teriyaki for some extra flavor.
Assorted raw vegetables: avocados lettuce, grated carrots, cucumber
Nori (seaweed) paper for rolling 2 pcs.
Wasabi
Soya sauce
Bamboo mat to use when rolling the sushi

**Instructions:**
Mix the sugar in a little warm water, pour onto the rice, and mix well. Place the bamboo mat on a towel, then place one nori roll on the bamboo. The shiny side of the nori should be facing down. Place a thin layer of the rice on the first part of the nori, the portion that is closest to you. Then place an assortment of vegetables in the middle of the rice. Not too many, or the rolls will be too thick. Roll the bamboo so that the part of the roll with rice on it rolls onto the nori, press to make a roll. Press the bamboo, so that the nori forms a roll. You can keep the rolls in the refrigerator, when you are ready to eat, cut the rolls using a sharp knife that is dipped in water. Serve the sushi with wasabi and soya sauce for dipping.

Serves 2 or 8 pieces

# Veggie Stir Fried Rice

This is a simple, easy recipe that can be made with white or brown rice, although we recommend brown!

**Ingredients:**

3 cups cooked rice, cooled
1 tbsp oil
2 tbsp soy sauce
Salt to taste
½ tsp pepper
1 tbsp veggie soup stock powder
1 cup chopped vegetables of your choice: greens, tomatoes, baby corn, green beans, snow peas, carrots, cauliflower
2 eggs (optional)

**Instructions:**

Heat the oil in a skillet or wok. Add the egg and cook until no longer translucent. Add the rice to the egg mixture, add the soy sauce, salt, pepper and veggie stock. Fry for 2-3 minutes until the rice is heated. Add the vegetables and cook for another 5 minutes, until the vegetables are slightly cooked.

Serves 2

# Orange & Veggie Couscous

We like to serve this flavorful recipe with falafel, yoghurt sauce, grilled veggies and chapatis.

**Ingredients:**

1 ½ cups couscous
4 cups water
2 tbsp olive oil
2 tsp grated orange rind
5 coriander pods
5 cloves
1 tbsp cinnamon powder
½ cup orange juice
1□3 cup raisins
½ cup chopped cabbage & baby corn (other vegetables can be substituted like pumpkin or spinach)
½ cup chopped, roasted cashews or almonds
¼ cup thinly sliced mint
Salt & pepper to taste

**Instructions:**

Heat the water to a boil, add the cinnamon powder. Put the cardamom and cloves into a tea ball, which can be retrieved, add them to the water. Add the couscous, olive oil, and the vegetables. Cook until tender around 10 minutes. Add the raisins and cashews. Cook another 1-2 minutes. Add the orange juice, mint, salt & pepper to taste.

Serves 2

# Indian Lemon Rice

This is a wonderful recipe brought to us by Sandya from Mysore. It is a simple recipe that yields a fragrant, tasty result.

**Ingredients:**

2 cups cooked basmati rice
Juice of 2 small lemons or limes
1 tsp mustard seeds
2 tbsp urad dahl (made from chick peas)
2 tbsp bengal dahl
2 green peppers, chopped into medium sized pieces
1 tbsp oil
1 tsp turmeric
Pinch of asafetida
Pinch of salt
Curry leaves
½ cup chopped fresh coriander
½ cup peanuts or cashews

**Instructions:**

Heat the ghee in a large saucepan. Add the mustard seeds. When the mustard seeds begin to pop, add the two types of dahl. Cook for 5 minutes on medium heat, taking care not to burn the dahl. Add the green peppers, asafetida, turmeric, curry leaves and salt. Continue to stir and cook for another 10 minutes. Remove from heat, add the lemon juice to the mixture and stir well. Add the rice and continue to stir. Put on medium heat. Add the chopped nuts and the coriander, stir well and serve.

Serves 2

# Indian Tomato Rice

**Ingredients:**
½ tsp Indian red chili powder
2 cups white basmati rice
4 cups water
2 cups chopped tomatoes
(optional: 1 onion, coarsely chopped)
1 tsp salt
1 tsp coriander powder
½ tsp turmeric
2 bay leaves
1 tbsp oil

Spice Mix: 4 cardamom pods, 1 cinnamon stick, 4 cloves, 2 tsp fennel ground together using mortar and pestle. Bunch of mint leaves, coriander leaves coarsely chopped

**Instructions:**
Heat oil in large saucepan. Add ½ of the ground spice mixture, bay leaves and fry in oil (if using onion, add to oil and sauté until soft). Add tomatoes, then add the remaining spices, turmeric and coriander. Cook the tomatoes 15-20 minutes, until they become soft and lose most of their form. Add the water and rice, coriander, and mint. Cover and cook until the water is absorbed and the rice is done.

Serves 2

# Vegetables

We recommend you use locally available organic greens and veggies in your home place for these recipes. These recipes use veggies we easily can get and grown on Koh Samui.

*Mixed Vegetable with Ginger Stir Fry*

# Mixed Vegetable with Ginger Stir Fry

Any stir fried vegetables can be used, and the recipe changed with the addition of ginger or cashew nuts.

**Ingredients:**

4 cups chopped vegetables
Any vegetable can be used be we typically use:
cabbage, kale, carrots, green beans, cauliflower
Fresh baby corn
½ cup chopped ginger
2 tbsp soy sauce (sweet and salty variety)
1 tsp veggie soup stock powder
½ tsp ground white pepper
½ cup cashew nuts (optional)
1 tbsp oil

**Instructions:**

Chop up vegetables into bite sized pieces. Heat 2-3 cups of water to boiling in large wok or saucepan. Cook the vegetables 5 minutes in the water. Drain the vegetables and the water. Heat ginger in oil in wok or saucepan. Sauté the ginger 2-3 minutes. Add the vegetables, soy sauce, veggie soup stock powder white pepper and cashew nuts. Stir rapidly and cook 5 minutes, until vegetables are just tender.

Serves 2

# Kale Stir fry

This recipe is made with the Thai version of kale, which are similar to what we find in the west, only the leaves are longer and they are less bitter. The kale could be substituted for another green, such as kohlrabi, spinach, brussels sprouts or mustard greens.

**Ingredients:**
8 cups of greens of your choice
1 cup water + pinch of salt
1 tbsp oil
2-4 tbsp soy sauce
½ tsp white pepper (optional)

**Instructions:**
Heat water and pinch of salt in wok or large sauce pan. When the water boils, add the greens. Cook the greens for 2-5 minutes, until tender. Cooking time will depend on the thickness of the type of green used. Drain the greens and set aside, discard the water. Heat oil in a wok or saucepan. Add the greens and sauté, add soy sauce, mix well. More soy sauce can be used, according to taste.

Serves 4

# Oven-Roasted Vegetables

This is a traditional Mediterranean recipe, which is simple yet delicious. It goes well with Falafel.

**Ingredients:**
We use these vegetables, because they are locally available. You could also use eggplant, green peppers, artichokes, zucchini (courgette) or pumpkin.
2 red peppers
2 yellow peppers
1 bunch of asparagus
Baby corn (optional)
3 tbsp olive oil
2 tbsp lemon juice
1 tbsp sea salt
1 tbsp crushed black pepper
2 tbsp each of rosemary & thyme. We use dried, however fresh would be preferable!

**Instructions:**
Mix the olive oil, herbs, lemon juice, salt, and pepper in a large bowl. Chop the peppers into strips, cut the hard ends from the asparagus. Mix the veggies with the oil and herbs until well coated. Line the veggies onto a baking pan, bake in a medium heat oven until slightly browned and soft for around 20 mintues.

Serves 2

# Pumpkin Stir Fry

This is a traditional Thai dish. It is normally served with egg. This makes it more of a main dish rather than an accompaniment. It is simple and delicious. If you can't get pumpkin, squash could be substituted.

**Ingredients:**

8 cups pumpkin, chopped into 1 inch chunks
Salt and white pepper to taste
1 tbsp veggie soup stock powder
1 tbsp oil
1 cup fresh basil leaves
3 eggs (optional)

**Instructions:**

Heat the oil, add the eggs to the oil, and cook until no longer translucent. Add the pumpkin, salt, pepper and veggie stock. Mix well and stir fry for 10 minutes, or until the pumpkin is soft (time will vary depending on the type of pumpkin). When the pumpkin is cooked, remove from heat, add the basil leaves and stir.

Serves 4

# Steamed Vegetables

This is a simple, yet delicious way to enjoy vegetables. If you can't find some of these vegetables, substitute with what is fresh and in season in your area. They are yummy with a little ghee sprinkled on top.

**Ingredients:**

Pumpkin – cut into large chunks (2 x 2 inches) 60 qr
Carrots – peeled and cut into 2 thick slices 60 qr
Green beans – cut into 3 inch pieces 60 qr
Greens of your choice 60 qr
Water for steaming

**Instructions:**

Use a large pot with a steamer (or a colander that fits inside). Fill pot with 2-3 inches of water. Put vegetables onto steamer, cook for 10 minutes until vegetables are tender. If you are preparing a large quantity of vegetables, they can be steamed separately.

Serves 2

# Indian Vegetable Subji

Subji is a mix of vegetables. There are many different types of subjis. Here are two of our favorites. Many of the subjis use a mix of spices that can be purchased at an Indian grocery store.

**Mixed Vegetable Subji**

8 cups of chopped vegetables such as beans, carrot, cauliflower, potato, snow peas
1 tsp ginger paste
1 green pepper finely chopped
½ cup cabbage chopped in long strips or 1 small onion coarsely chopped
Red chili powder (to taste, start with a pinch, increase as you can)
1 tbsp Pav bhaji masala powder
1 tsp tomato puree or one chopped tomato
1 tsp salt
1 tbsp oil

**Instructions:**

Cook the vegetables in a large pot of salted water for 10-15 minutes, until soft. Drain the water and set aside. Heat the oil in a large pot or skillet, add the green pepper and cabbage (or onion) and fry until soft. Add the red chili powder and the pau bhaji masala. Add the tomato puree or chopped tomato and fry until the tomato is soft. Add the vegetables and cook for 10 minutes.

Serves 4

# Chickpea & Cauliflower Subji

**Ingredients:**

8 cups of chopped potato and cauliflower
1 tsp chopped ginger
1 tsp coriander powder
1 tsp cumin powder
1 green pepper finely chopped
Red chili powder (to taste, start with a pinch, increase as you can!)
Chole or channa masala (for cooking chick peas)
1 cup cooked chickpeas
1 tomato
1 tsp salt
1 tbsp oil

**Instructions:**

Heat the oil in a large pot or skillet, add the green pepper and fry until soft. Add the turmeric, cumin, coriander, chili powder, channa masala, ginger, mix well and fry for 1 minute. Add the tomato and salt. After the tomato is soft, add the cooked chickpeas, cauliflower, and potato. Cook until the vegetables are soft, around 20 minutes. You can add a little butter or ghee at the end, or around 1 tsp of cashew powder (be careful, this can thicken the sauce).

Serves 4

# Indian-Style Potatoes with Tomatoes

**Ingredients:**

5 potatoes
2 tomatoes
Pinch of asafetida
1 tbsp finely chopped fresh ginger
1 tbsp cumin seeds
1 tsp turmeric
Salt to taste
Handful of chopped fresh coriander
1 tbsp ghee
1 green chili (optional)

**Instructions:**

Boil the potatoes, until just cooked, remove the skin and chop. Heat the ghee in a large skillet, add the asafetida, ginger, cumin seeds. When they are brown, add the tumeric and salt. Add the tomatoes, mix well and heat through. Add the potatoes, mix in around one cup of water, so the mixture is a little soupy. Cook for 5-10 minutes. Add the green chili at the end of cooking.

Serves 2

# Potato & Green Bean Subji

This is an easy delicious recipe, full of wonderful Indian flavours.

**Ingredients:**
2 large potatoes or 4 small potatoes
8 cups of green beans (we use the long variety)
2 tbsp oil
Two pinches of asafetida
1 tbsp cumin seeds
1 tbsp coriander powder
1 tbsp turmeric
1 tsp salt
1 cup water

**Instructions:**
Boil the potatoes ahead of time, remove the skin. Heat ghee in a large skillet or wok and add the asafetida. Let it simmer for 1-2 minutes, add the cumin, tumeric, and coriander powder. Cook the spices until the cumin seeds start to brown. Add the beans and the potatoes and salt. Then add the water. Cover and let cook, stir the mixture every five minutes.

Serves 2

# Salads and Dressings

*Vietnamese Summer Rolls with Tamarind Sauce*

# Vietnamese Summer Rolls

**Ingredients:**
Makes 10 summer rolls
10-15 sheets of rice paper (a few to spare just in case)
1 cup chopped mint
1 cup chopped lettuce
1 cup chopped carrot
1 cup chopped basil
1 cup chopped coriander
Around 20 green beans, cooked for 2 minutes in boiling water
1 ½ cups thin glass noodles, cooked in salted water until tender

**For the tamarind sauce:**
½ cup tamarind fruit
½ cup chopped coriander
2 tbsp honey
Salt to taste
1 cup water
½ cup peanuts

**Instructions:**
Put the tamarind fruit in small bowl, cover with boiling water. Let sit 10 minutes, stir to break up the tamarinds from the seeds. Drain the seeds and bits of tamarind from the water. Cook the salt, and tamarind for ½ hour together. Dry roast the peanuts in a pan, then chop. Add chopped coriander and peanuts to the sauce. Cool before serving and then add honey.

**How to roll:**
Dip rice paper into warm water until soft
Lay on a flat surface and add a bit of each of the ingredients
Roll, starting with the side that is closest to you, about half way
Fold each of the sides inward, like wrapping a present
Continue to roll, until reaching the other edge
Cover with plastic wrap to keep air from drying the rice paper

Serves 10 rolls

# Sweet Potato Salad

**Ingredients:**
4 cup sweet potato
1 cup green pepper
¼ cup coriander

**For the sauce:**
1 tbsp olive oil
1 tbsp honey
1 tsp salt and black pepper
1 tsp vinegar
½ tsp yellow mustard

**Instructions:**
Cut sweet potato into 1 inch square. Cut bell pepper into ¼ inch small pieces. Boil potato with water for 15 mins until cooked. Drain water and wait for potato until cool. Mix the sauce until blended nicely. Mix potato with sauce and coriander evenly. Serve at room temperature or allow to cool.

Serves 2

# "Som Tom" Thai Papaya Salad

Som Tom is a favorite of many of our guests. If you cannot find green papaya, you could use grated carrots instead.

**Ingredients:**

2-3 green chilies
½ cup lime juice
2 tomatoes chopped in wedges (around ½ cup)
½ cup green beans
¼ cup honey
1 cup grated carrots
4 cups grated green papaya
1 tsp white pepper
2-4 tbsp sweet soy sauce
2 tbsp peanuts

**Instructions:**

Grind chilies with mortar and pestle, or in food processor. Add green beans and the lime juice, continue to grind. Add honey, soy sauce, tomatoes, and grind more. Add white pepper and peanuts, and continue to grind. Gradually add the sauce to the papaya and carrots. Mix well and pound the papaya and carrot with the pestle. The mixing and beating infuses the flavor of the sauce into the papaya.

Serves 2

# "Yum Yai" Thai Green & Veggie Salad

**Ingredients:**
1/3 cup carrot
1/3 cup Chinese cabbage
¼ cup mint leaves
¼ cup coriander
2 tbsp crushed peanut and cashew nut
1/3 cup tomatoes
3 green lettuce
1/4 cup onion

**Salad dressing:**
1 chili
1 tbsp coriander root
2 tbsp soy sauce
2 tbsp honey
2 tbsp lemon juice
1 tbsp vinegar
¼ teaspoon sea salt

**Instructions:**
To make the salad dressing, blend together chili and coriander root for about 2 minutes or until smooth. Add the rest of the ingredients. Put aside. Just before serving, mix the salad dressing ingredients together in a bowl. Then, pour in the dressing and toss for 2-3 minutes.

Serves 1

# Cucumber, Coconut & Mung Salad

This is a delicious, simple salad brought to us by Sandya.

**Ingredients:**
4 cups chopped cucumber
½ cup shredded coconut
½ cup mung beans, soaked for 1 hour
1 cup chopped coriander
3 tbsp lime juice or juice of one lime
Salt to taste

**For the dressing:**
½ tsp mustard seed
1 tbsp ghee
Pinch of asafetida
Heat the ghee, add the mustard seeds. When they begin to pop, add the asafetida. Cook for one minute.

**Instructions:**
Mix the cucumber, coconut, mung together. Add the lime juice, coriander and salt to taste. Add the dressing and stir well.

Serves 2

# Carrot, Coconut & Sprout Salad

**Ingredients:**
4 cups of grated carrots
½ cup coconut
1 cup soaked mung beans (for at least 1 hour)
3 tbsp lime juice or juice of 1 lime
Salt to taste

**For the dressing:**
1 tbsp mustard seed
1 tbsp ghee
Pinch of asafetida
Heat the ghee and add the mustard seeds. When they begin to pop, add the asafetida. Cook for one minute.

**Instructions:**
Mix the carrot, coconut, mung together. Add the lime juice salt to taste. Add the dressing and stir well.

Serves 2

# Vinaigrette Salad Dressing

This is a simple yet tasty vinaigrette dressing brought by Jessica from France, goes well on most salads. It can keep for several days in the fridge.

**Ingredients:**
1 tbsp Dijon mustard
4 tbsp olive oil
2 tbsp balsamic vinegar
Salt and pepper to taste.
Optional ingredients: fresh parsley, crushed garlic, cayenne pepper, mustard seeds

**Instructions:**
Mix the oil and the mustard together nicely. Add the vinegar and mix well. Add salt and pepper to taste.

# Black Sesame Dressing

**Ingredients:**
1 tbsp lemon juice
1 tbsp soya sauce
½ tbsp black sesame seeds
½ tbsp sesame oil

**Instructions:**
Mix lemon juice and soya sauce together. Then add sesame oil. Stir in black sesame seeds and mix nicely. If making larger portion, you can add hot water to dilute it slightly.

# Simple Olive Oil Dressing

This is a nice dressing which doesn't contain vinegar, so it won't aggrevate Pitta dosha.

**Ingredients:**
2 tbsps olive oil
1 tbsp lemon juice
Dash of Bragg's Amino Acids
Pinch of sea salt & black pepper
Optional – one chopped green chili

**Instructions:**
Mix lemon juice and soya sauce together. Then add sesame oil. Stir in black sesame seeds and mix nicely. If making larger portion, you can add hot water to dilute it slightly.

# Tahini Lime Dressing

**Ingredients:**
3 tbsp white sesame seeds (more if you want more paste)
2 tbsp lemon juice
2 tbsp soya sauce
1 tbsp sesame oil
Hot water
Pinch of salt

**Instructions:**
Roast sesame seeds in a pan. Use a blender to mix roasted sesame seeds and salt to make Tahini paste. Slowly add a little hot water and lemon juice to the paste until you get a good watery consistency. Add the soya sauce and sesame oil to the dressing. Mix well.

## Notes:

# Desserts

*Mango Sticky Rice*

# Mango Sticky Rice

This is an extremely popular Thai dessert. We made the coconut milk ourselves, but you can used canned coconut milk instead.

**Ingredients:**
1 ¾ cups coconut milk
¾ cups coconut milk for the sweet sauce
2 cups sticky rice, or short grained white rice
1 cup of brown sugar, this is a rough estimate, you add sugar to your taste
2-3 tsp salt
4-5 ripe mangoes

**Instructions:**
Soak the rice overnight in water. Wash the rice twice. Put the rice in a steamer. We use a pot made for steaming, with a piece of cloth over the pot to keep the rice from running through the holes. Steam the rice for thirty minutes, until it is no longer grainy in texture when eaten. While the rice is cooking, heat around ¾ cup of coconut milk in a small pot. Heat the coconut milk slowly, gradually add brown sugar until the mixture starts to thicken. This sauce will be eaten with the sticky rice and mango. With the remaining coconut milk, add 1-2 tsp salt, and roughly ½ cup of sugar. This mixture will be very sweet. Gradually add the sugar, stirring well to dissolve the sugar in the coconut milk. When the sticky rice is done, put into a large bowl. While hot, add the unheated coconut milk to the rice. Continue to add the coconut milk and stir until the rice is coated and sweet enough. Peel the mangoes, slice close to each side of the seed, then gut again into small strips. Serve with the coconut milk sauce on the side.

Serves 8

# Energy Balls

**Ingredients:**
1 cup roasted sesame seed
½-2 cups peanut butter (for peanut allergies substitute almond butter)
½ cup honey
½ cup dry roasted coconut
½ cup soft dried fruit (raisins, cranberry, dates, cherries, currants)
½ cup nuts, seeds (whatever you prefer)
1 tbsp spirulina

**Instructions:**
Thoroughly mix all ingredients into large bowl. The consistency should be somewhat thick and able to bind together. If too soft, add more dry ingredients. If too dry, add more fruit, nut butter or honey.

Take a small scoop and roll into a ball, (about the size of a golf ball) or press into a pan for squares. Put in refrigerator for 2 hours. Then serve, or freeze!

Makes 4 balls

# Swedish Choco-Oat Balls

These rich, chocolate treats, brought to us by Ulrica from Stockholm, have quickly become a favorite at Samahita Retreat. They are easy to make and sure to please.

**Ingredients:**

½ cup butter (softened)
1 cup honey
3 ¾ cups oatmeal
2 tbsp cocoa powder
1 tsp vanilla sugar
1 tbsp water
1 tbsp strong coffee
Grated coconut for rolling the balls

**Instructions:**

Mix the dry ingredients into the butter (honey, oatmeal , cocoa), mixing until there are no lumps left in the butter. Add the water and coffee into the dough, mix again. The dough should be not to hard or soft, yet hard enough to be rolled into small balls (around 3 cm, or 1 inch in diameter). Roll the dough into balls, then roll in coconut shavings. Store in the freezer, take out 20 minutes before serving.

Makes 6 balls

# Cashew Nut Cup

**Ingredients:**

1 cup cashew nuts
1 cup raisins
2 tbsp strawberry jam
2 tbsp honey
2 bars of plain dark chocolate

**Instructions:**

This was brought to us by Clare (Paul's sister) adapted from a recipe his mother would make. Roast the cashew nuts over medium flame. In a separate pot, melt chocolate over low flame. Stir in orange marmalade, cashew nuts, raisins. Turn off flame, add honey. Stir nicely in pot until chocolate coats mixture evenly. Put into small individual paper cups for serving. Put in fridge for 1-2 hours for chocolate to harden.

Makes 4 cups

# Guilt-Free Chocolate Balls

If you crave sugar in the afternoon, this is a great substitute for refined sugar.

**Ingredients:**
2 cups dates
2 cups raisins
1 cup sunflower seeds
¼ cup black or white sesame seeds
2-3 tbsp cocoa powder
Oil to facilitate grinding seeds
Ground up peanuts, cocoa powder or sesame for rolling

**Instructions:**
Soak the dried fruits for a couple hours. Chop them up then mix. Grind the sunflower seeds & sesame seeds in a blender. Add a little oil (sesame or any vegetable oil) to aid in mixing. Mix all ingredients together and form into balls. You can roll them in a ground nut like peanuts, sesame seeds, coconut or in cocoa powder.

Makes 8 balls

# Blueberry Crumble

This is a wonderful dessert, brought to us from Louisiana by Jessica's mom, Zoe. Any fruit can be used, apple, blueberries, blackberries, and even pineapple.

**Ingredients:**

For the topping:
2 cups uncooked rolled oats
1 cup whole meal flour
1 cup firmly packed brown sugar
¾ cup butter
1 tbsp cinnamon powder

**For the fruit:**

2 cups blueberries or any fruit you desire
1 tbsp flour
½ cup brown sugar
2 tbsp lemon juice
½ to ¾ cup water
Dash of salt

**For the topping:**

Mix rolled oats, flour and brown sugar. Add melted butter and mix well. Line bottom of a pan, (8 inches or 12 centimeters around the size for a cake) with the oatmeal mixture, reserving ¾ cup for the topping.

**Instructions:**

Combine the remaining ingredients in a saucepan: fruit, flour, sugar, lemon juice, water and a dash of salt. Cook on low heat for 5 minutes. Remove from heat and pour into the pan with the crust. Sprinkle with the topping that was set aside. Bake at 350 degrees F (175 degrees C) for 35 minutes, until the topping is slightly browned and the crumble is a little bit firm. We like to serve with some yoghurt for a sauce!

Serves 4

# Choc-Oat Chip Cookies

**Ingredients:**

1¾ cups whole meal flour
1 tsp baking soda
½ tsp salt (optional)
1¼ cups firmly packed brown sugar
1 cup butter (softened)
2 eggs
2 tbsp milk
2 tsp vanilla extract
2½ cups quick or whole oats
2 cups chocolate chips (we like semi-sweet variety)
1 cups chopped nuts (optional)

**Instructions:**

Combine flour, baking soda, and salt in small bowl. Beat brown sugar and butter in large bowl until creamy. Beat in eggs, milk and vanilla extract. Gradually beat in flour mixture. Stir in oats, chocolate chips and nuts, mix well. Drop by rounded tablsespoon onto an ungreased baking sheet. Bake in pre-heated oven of 375 degrees F (190 degrees C) Bake for 9-10 minutes for gooey cookies, and 12-13 minutes for crispier cookies.

Make 24 pieces

# Whole Wheat Shortbread Cookies

**Ingredients:**
1¼ cup butter
½ cup brown sugar
1 tsp vanilla
¼ tsp sea salt
2 tbsp ghee
3 cups whole wheat flour
4 tbsp chocolate chip (optional)

**Instructions:**
In a bowl, mix together melted butter and brown sugar. Add in vanilla, sea salt and ghee. Mix the mixture until smooth. Put the mixture into a cookie cutter to make round shapes. Keep in fridge until the cookie is in shape. Set the oven at 300 degrees F, bake the cookies for 30 minutes or until golden brown.

Make 10 pieces

# Vegan Cookies

These are fantastic cookies that are pure vegan from Lesley in Canada.

**Ingredients:**

1 firm tofu (8 oz)
2½ cups brown sugar
¾ cups vegetable oil
2 cups oats
2 tsp vanilla
2 cups of raisins and/or chocolate chips and/or coconut

**Instructions:**

Mash up the tofu, if you have a hand mixer this helps. Add the oil and sugar and mix well until smooth. Add the vanilla, then gradually add the oats. Add the raisins, chocolate chips, coconut.
Bake at 275 degrees F (130 degrees C) for 30 minutes.

Make 10 pieces

# "The Best Ever Carrot Cake"

This recipe comes to us from the U.S. We used cashew nuts instead of walnuts, which works just fine.

**Ingredients:**

6 cups grated carrots, ½ cup chopped ginger
1 cup brown sugar
1 cup raisins
4 eggs
1 ½ cup brown sugar
1 cup vegetable oil
2 teaspoons vanilla extract
1 cup crushed pineapple
3 cups whole meal flour
1 ½ tsp baking soda
1 tsp salt
4 tsp ground cinnamon
1 cup chopped walnuts
Cream cheese frosting (recipe below)

**Instructions:**

In a medium bowl, combine grated carrots and brown sugar. Set aside for 60 minutes, then add the raisins. Preheat the oven to 350 degrees F. Grease and flour one large cake pan, or two smaller round cake pans. In a large bowl, beat the eggs until light. Gradually beat in the sugar, oil, and vanilla. Stir in the pineapple. Combine the flour, baking soda, salt and cinnamon and then stir into the wet mixture until absorbed. Finally stir in the carrot mixture and the walnuts. Pour evenly into the prepared pans. Bake for 45 to 50 minutes in the oven. Cake is done when a toothpick inserted into the center comes out clean. Cool for 10 minutes before removing from the pan. When completely cooled, spread on the cream cheese frosting.

## Cream Cheese Frosting

This frosting goes very well with the carrot cake.

**Ingredients:**

2 cups of cream cheese (softened)
½ cup butter (softened)
2 cups powdered sugar
1 tsp vanilla extract

In medium sized bowl, mix together the cream cheese and butter until creamy. Mix the vanilla, then gradually stir in the powdered sugar.

Serves 6

# "All Equal Cake"

This is a very simple cake to make, brought to us by Petra from Austria. You can put almost any kind of cut fruit on top. In Austria, they mostly use apples, apricots and plums. Nuts can also be used, all kind are good, such as almonds hazelnuts or walnuts. All should be cut into little pieces; chocolate chips or raisins are also fine. The amount should be a handful. You can combine all fruits, nuts or others as you like. For example apples with raisins, apricots with almonds, mangoes with cashew, chocolate with raisins and so on.....

**Ingredients:**
3 eggs
Butter
Brown sugar
Fruits nuts whole meal (All divided equally)
Flour

**Instructions:**
Weigh the eggs. Take the same weight of butter, sugar and flour. Put butter in a bowl and beat it until it is creamy. Add sugar in little portions and keep beating the dough. Add one egg at a time and keep beating the mixture. Add the flour in small portions and keep beating the dough. Peel and cut fruit and nuts. Put butter in the cake pan, all around and a little flour to cover the butter. Add the dough to the cake pan. If you like, put nuts or chocolate chips on top. The fruit will sink into the cake; that is okay!

Bake in oven at 375 degrees F for approximately 45 minutes. Insert a toothpick into the cake, if it comes out clean it is done.

Serves 4

# Yoghurt Cake

**Ingredients:**
3 eggs
1 cup brown sugar
1 cup yoghurt
½ cup vegetable oil
2 cups whole meal flour
1 teaspoon baking powder
Dash of salt

**Instructions:**
Put the eggs into a bowl, and beat until they are creamy and a little fluffy. Gradually add the sugar, bit by bit and keep beating into the dough. Add the yoghurt, and keep beating into the dough. Add the oil in small portions, and keep beating the dough. Gradually add the flour and the baking powder, keep beating while you are adding. Peel and cut fruit and nuts to your liking (as with the "All equal cake"). Grease the cake pan with butter and sprinkle a thin layer of flour on top. Add the dough to the cake pan. If you like, put nuts or chocolate chips on top. The fruit will sink into the cake; that is okay!

Bake in oven at 375 degrees F for approximately 45 minutes. Insert a toothpick into the cake, if it comes out clean it is done.

Serves 4

# Vegan Chocolate Cake

This recipe is brought to us by Chef Ellen who shared many of her scrumptious desserts on her visit. This was a huge favorite.

**Ingredients:**

2 cups whole meal flour
2 cups brown sugar
½ cup cocoa powder
1 ½ tbsp baking soda
1 tbsp salt
½ tbsp vegetable oil
1 ½ tbsp vanilla
1 ½ tbsp vinegar (prefer apple cider)
1 ¼ tbsp very strong coffee (prepared)
1 cup water or soy milk

**Instructions:**

Mix all ingredients together and pour into a greased baking pan. Bake at 350 degrees F for 45 minutes. Drizzle with cocoa powder before serving.

**Non Vegan option, finish with chocolate sauce made of dark chocolate and milk.

Serves 4

## Notes:

**Notes:**